PRINCIPLES OF

CHURCH LIFE

PRINCIPLES OF
CHURCH LIFE

Bill Scheidler
with Dick Iverson &
Kevin J. Conner

Published by City Christian Publishing
9200 NE Fremont • Portland, Oregon 97220

Printed in the United States of America

City Christian Publishing is a ministry of City Bible Church and is dedicated to serving the local church and its leaders through the production and distribution of quality equipping resources. It is our prayer that these materials, proven in the context of the local church, will equip leaders in exalting the Lord and extending His kingdom.

For a free catalog of additional resources from City Christian Publishing, please call 1-800-777-6057 or visit our web site at *www.CityChristianPublishing.com*.

Principles of Church Life
© Copyright 1976 by Bill Scheidler
ISBN 0-914936-23-9

INTRODUCTION

We are living in a day when it is absolutely critical that believers know what they believe and that what they believe is firmly based on the Word of God, the Bible. So many believers today are enlisting in the army of the Lord without the sword of the Spirit and they find themselves unarmed when it comes to doing spiritual battle.

This manual is designed to give every believer a foundational understanding of the basic *Principles of Church Life.* It is designed to assist the believer in inspecting their personal foundation in the Lord and ensuring that none of the basic building blocks of victorious Christian living are missing.

It was also designed as a membership course for Bible Temple in Portland, Oregon. All of those who would become members of the church must go through this course so that they can all be of one mind and purpose in the following of the Lord.

Many pastors today are finding a similar need to instruct their people in the basics the Christian life. We have therefore made this manual available for a wider use and distribution. This book may be used in two specific ways:

1. As a personal study manual. By reading through the material and looking up the various Bible references the student of the word will be built up and encouraged in the faith.

2. As a membership manual for churches. By going through the material together as a class a pastor can feed his people the foundations of the faith, line upon line.

The text of this manual follows a simple question and answer format with occasional spaces where key words or thoughts have been left out of the text. The key to these blanks is found in the back of the manual. These answer sheets have been perforated on the inside margin so that they can be removed for the class presentation. For personal study the answer key may be consulted as the student progresses through the manual.

Our prayer is that God will use this manual to strengthen His Church that the Church might become all that God has intended for it to be.

Bill Scheidler

Principles Of
CHURCH LIFE

Table of Contents

1

Why Study Doctrine?

Purpose: The purpose of this lesson is to help us to see our need for teaching and biblical instruction and to develop a desire to go on with the Lord — beyond a mere confession of faith. A deeper understanding of what we believe and why we believe it will produce a greater maturity and an increased fruitfulness in the life of the believer.

Key Verse: "That we henceforth be no more children, tossed to and fro, and carried about with every wind of doctrine, by the sleight of men, and cunning craftiness, whereby they lie in wait to deceive; but speaking the truth in love, may grow up into Him in all things, which is the head, even Christ." Ephesians 4:14, 15 KJV

I. WHAT IS DOCTRINE?

A. The word "doctrine" simply means _____ or

_____ .

B. A "biblical doctrine" is simply all that the Bible teaches or says about a particular subject.

II. WHAT IS THE BASIC PURPOSE OF ALL DOCTRINAL STUDY?

Luke, the author of the third Gospel, put it this way, ". . . to set forth in order a declaration of those things which are most surely believed among us . . . that thou mightest know the certainty of those things, wherein thou hast been instructed." Luke 1:1, 4

The purpose for all doctrinal study is fivefold:

A. To equip the believer to do _____ .

"All scripture is given by inspiration of God, and is profitable for doctrine, for reproof, for correction, for instruction in righteousness: that the man of God may be perfect, throughly furnished unto all good works." II Timothy 3:16, 17

B. To prepare the believer to war _____ warfare against Satan.

C. To ground our faith _____ on the Word of Truth.

"Rooted and built up in Him, and stablished in the faith, as ye have been taught, abounding therein with thanksgiving." Colossians 2:7

D. To enable the believer to properly _____ to the Lord and His people.

"But the goal of our instruction is love from a pure heart and a good conscience and a sincere faith." I Timothy 1:5 (NAS)

"Seeing ye have purified your souls in obeying the truth through the Spirit unto unfeigned love of the brethren, see that ye love one another with a pure heart fervently;"   I Peter 1:22

E. To instruct the believer as to how to _____ in the House of the Lord.

"These things write I unto thee . . . that thou mayest know how thou oughtest to behave thyself in the house of God, which is the church of the living God, the pillar and ground of the truth." I Timothy 3:14, 15

III. WHY IS IT IMPORTANT FOR EVERY BELIEVER TO HAVE A GOOD BIBLICAL FOUNDATION?

Many people today would lead us to believe that it does not matter what you believe as long as you have accepted Christ as your saviour. The Bible is emphatic about this point that it is important that every believer knows what they believe and why they believe it (I Timothy 6:1-4; Titus 2:7-15; I Timothy 4:6, 13).

". . . Take heed unto thyself, and unto the doctrine; continue in them: for in doing this thou shalt both save thyself, and them that hear thee." I Timothy 4:16

There are several reasons why it is important to know what we believe:

A. Because the last days will be characterized by _____ . This is very apparent in our day with the rise of various cults and the infiltration of secular, humanistic philosophies (I Timothy 4:1, 2; II John 7; Matthew 24:10-13, 24).

". . . Take heed that no man deceive you. For many shall come in my name saying, I am Christ; and shall deceive many." Matthew 24:4, 5

B. Because every believer is to _____ others to observe the commandments of the Lord.

"Go ye therefore, and teach all nations . . . teaching them to observe all things whatsoever I have commanded you." Matthew 28:19, 20

C. Because all believers should be able to give _____ when questioned concerning the hope that they have in Christ.

". . . Be ready always to give _____ that asketh you a reason of the hope that is in you with meekness and fear." I Peter 3:15

D. Because what we believe will affect _____ (John 14:6; II Peter 1:8-11).

". . . the holy scriptures which are able to make thee wise unto salvation . . ." II Timothy 3:15

IV. WHAT ARE THE REQUIREMENTS FOR DOCTRINE?

A. Doctrine must be _____ (I Timothy 1:10; II Timothy 4:3, 4).

"But speak thou the things which become sound doctrine." Titus 2:1

B. Doctrine must be _____ (Titus 2:7, 8).

C. Doctrine must be based on _____ (II Timothy 3:14-17).

"Knowing this first, that no prophecy of the scripture is of any private interpretation. For the prophecy came not in old time by the will of man: but holy men of God spake as they were moved by the Holy Ghost." II Peter 1:20, 21

D. Doctrine must be mixed with _____ (I Thessalonians 2:13).

"For unto us was the gospel preached, as well as unto them: but the word preached did not profit them, not being mixed with faith in them that heard it." Hebrews 4:2

E. Doctrine must be _____ (Romans 6:17; Luke 11:28).

"But be ye doers of the word, and not hearers only, deceiving your own selves. For if any be a hearer of the word, and not a doer, he is like unto a man beholding his natural face in a glass: for he beholdeth himself, and goeth his way, and straightway forgetteth what manner of man he was. But whoso looketh into the perfect law of liberty, and continueth therein, he being not a forgetful hearer, but a doer of the work, this man shall be blessed in his deed." James 1:22-25

Conclusion: God is raising up a body of people in our day who are going to go beyond the last generation in entering into the provisions of the New Covenant. If this is true, we must be a people who have a love for the Word of Truth and a desire to learn the right ways of God. We are living in a time where people like to choose for themselves what they want to hear and are resisting some of the things that are clearly revealed in the Word of God. If we will distinguish ourselves in these days by a love for righteousness and a desire to live by God's Word, God will do special things through us as He has promised.

Psalm 19:7-11

The law of the Lord is perfect, converting the soul:
The testimony of the Lord is sure, making wise the simple.
The statutes of the Lord are right, rejoicing the heart:
The commandment of the Lord is pure, enlightening the eyes.
The fear of the Lord is clean, enduring forever:
The judgements of the Lord are true and righteous altogether.
More to be desired are they than gold, yea, than much fine gold:
Sweeter also than honey and the honeycomb.
Moreover by them is thy servant warned:
And in keeping of them there is great reward.

2

Repentance From Dead Works

Purpose: The purpose of this lesson is to help us to recognize that the only true foundation on which to begin to build the Christian life and by which to maintain it is that of repentance from everything that hinders us from becoming all that God desires for us to become.

Key Verse: ". . . The time is fulfilled, and the kingdom of God is at hand: repent ye, and believe the Gospel." Mark 1:15 KJV

I. WHAT IS THE FIRST WORD OF THE GOSPEL?

The first word of the Gospel is _____ . The second word of

the Gospel is _____ (Mark 1:15).

A. The message John the Baptist gave to prepare the world for the coming of Jesus was

_____ (Matthew 3:1-8).

B. The first message that Jesus proclaimed as a prerequisite for entering the Kingdom

was _____ (Matthew 4:17).

C. The message that the disciples carried wherever they went was the message of

_____ (Mark 6:7-13).

D. The call that went out on the first sermon after the outpouring of the Spirit was of

_____ (Acts 2:38, 39).

E. Paul began his preaching with the message of _____ (Acts 20:20, 21).

". . . repentance and remission of sins should be preached in his name among all nations, beginning at Jerusalem." Luke 24:47

"And the times of this ignorance God winked at; but now commandeth all men everywhere to repent." Acts 17:30

Repentance is the first step in the believer's life. God commands it. If this foundation is not properly laid, the whole structure will be shaky, unable to stand the tests and trials that come (Luke 6:46-49). The Psalmist declares, "If the foundations be destroyed, what can the righteous do?" (Psalm 11:3). We must firmly lay this "foundation of repentance from dead works" if we are to be strong (Hebrews 6:1-2).

II. WHAT DOES IT MEAN FOR A PERSON TO "REPENT"?

A. The word "repent" means to change one's mind, thought, purpose or views regarding a

matter. It refers to a change in _____ , which results in a new direction for the whole life.

B. Charles Finney defined repentance as an "intellectual and a hearty giving up of all controversy with God upon all and every point. It implies a conviction that God is wholly right, and the sinner is wholly wrong, and a thorough and hearty abandonment of all _____."

III. WHY IS REPENTANCE NECESSARY FOR MAN?

A. Because of the _____ , the first man, into sin there is an inborn desire in the mind of man to go his own way and rebel against the right ways of God (Ephesians 2:3; Colossians 1:21).

"There is a way which seemeth right unto a man, but the end thereof are the ways of death." Proverbs 14:12

"All we like sheep have gone astray; we have turned everyone to his own way; and the Lord hath laid on him the iniquity of us all." Isaiah 53:6

B. Because _____ has erred from the right ways of God by virtue of his own decisions in life   (Romans 7:18-25).

"For all have sinned, and come short of the glory of God." Romans 3:23

C. Because _____ man does not have the power to live a life that is pleasing to God (Hebrews 11:6).

IV. WHAT ARE SOME OF THE WRONG CONCEPTS ABOUT REPENTANCE?

There are many concepts that have been confused with true repentance. The tragedy is that if we accept any one of these false concepts it will keep us from experiencing genuine repentance.

True repentance is not:

A. _____ . Conviction of sin will always precede genuine repentance, but not all who are convicted will truly repent (Acts 24:24, 25).

B. _____ . Worldly sorrow is simply being sorry for "getting caught", but not being sorry for the actual crime committed. Given the same set of circumstances this person would probably repeat the same sin (II Corinthians 7:10).

C. _____ . Reformation in this sense is simply trying to "turn over a new leaf" in the strength of the natural man. This will never be successful without a genuine heart change.

D. _____ . The Pharisees in Christ's day were very religious but they were hypocrites. It is possible to maintain a form of religion but never experience the genuine power of repentance (II Timothy 3:5).

E. _____ , or "only believism". Mental faith is merely the mental acceptance and assent to a set of creeds or doctrines, but without any real change of heart and life (James 2:19, 20).

Oswald Chambers writes that repentance "describes that deep and radical change whereby a sinner turns from the idols of self and sin to God, and devotes every movement of the inner and outer man to the captivity of His obedience."

V. WHAT ARE THE FRUITS OF GENUINE REPENTANCE?

If genuine repentance has taken place on the inside of man there will be outward signs, or fruits, of this inward work. Although no one can judge the heart of another, there should be external evidence that the heart has been truly changed. John the Baptist did not merely accept the Pharisee's confession that they desired a baptism unto repentance, he challenged them to also "bring forth therefore fruits meet for repentance." Matthew 3:8

If genuine repentance has taken place, it should be evidenced by the following:

A. A godly sorrow for sin (II Corintians 7:9-11).

B. A confession of sin and a plea for mercy (I John 1:9; Luke 15:21; 18:13, 14).

C. A turning from, or forsaking, of sinful ways (Proverbs 28:13; Acts 19:17-20).

D. A godly hatred for sin (Ezekiel 36:31-33).

E. A turning unto the ways of righteousness (I Thessalonians 1:9; Colossians 3:1-14).

F. A restitution for the wrongs done, wherever possible (Leviticus 6:1-7; Luke 19:8).

Without these fruits being manifest, there is no genuine Bible repentance.

VI. WHAT ARE THE RESULTS OF GENUINE REPENTANCE?

A. There is great joy in Heaven (Luke 15:7, 10).

B. There is a pardon and remission of sins (Isaiah 55:7).

C. There is great refreshing from the Lord (Acts 3:19-21).

D. There is a clearing of the conscience (II Corinthians 7:10-11).

Conclusion: Repentance is something that is absolutely necessary if we are to be founded on the Rock, Christ Jesus. It begins as a one-time experience when we accept the Lordship of Christ in our life, but it continues to be important in the process of sanctification as the Holy Spirit is faithful to point out many other areas that are in need of change. Every believer needs to be prepared to respond in repentance as often as there is a need for it. In this way we will progress daily in our Christian walk toward God's ultimate will for our lives.

3

Faith Toward God

Purpose: The purpose of this lesson is to help us to see that the Christian life is a life of faith — not a dead faith, but a faith that is alive and active, responding quickly to the Word of the Lord.

Key Verse: "But without faith it is impossible to please Him: for he that cometh to God must believe that He is, and that He is a rewarder of them that diligently seek Him." Hebrews 11:6 KJV

I. HOW IMPORTANT IS FAITH?

A. Faith toward God is the second principle of the Doctrine of Christ. (Hebrews 6:1).

B. Faith and repentance are inseparably linked together. They are mutually _____

_____ upon each other (Acts 20:21; Mark 1:15).

E. Baxter puts it this way: "To profess to turn to God without forsaking sin in repentance ends in hypocrisy. To attempt to forsake sin without turning to God in faith, ends in failure and despair."

C. Faith is the foundation for the entire Christian life. Nothing can be known or received from God unless man first believes in His existence and, secondly, that God has revealed Himself in His Word, the Bible (Hebrews 11:6).

"The just shall live by _____ ." Romans 1:17

II. WHAT IS FAITH?

A. The Bible defines faith in Hebrews 11:1, "Now faith is being sure of what we hope for and certain of what we do not see." (NIV)

B. The dictionary defines faith as a "trust, firm persuasion, assurance, firm conviction, confidence in another and another's word."

C. Charles Finney put it this way: Faith is "a receiving of Christ for just what He is represented to be in His Gospel, and an unqualified surrender of the will, and of the whole being to Him."

D. R. A. Torrey states, "To believe God is to rely upon or have unhesitating assurance of the truth of God's testimony, even though it is unsupported by any other evidence, and to rely upon or have unfaltering assurance of the fulfillment of His promises, even though everything seen seems against fulfillment."

III. WHAT IS THE SOURCE OF TRUE FAITH?

A. The only source of true biblical faith is _____
   (Romans 10:4-17).

   "So then faith cometh by hearing, and hearing by the Word of God." Romans 10:17

B. Abraham serves as an example to us of how to receive and respond to the Word of God (Hebrews 11:8-12; Romans 4:16-22).

   The manner in which Abraham manifests faith is the manner in which we must manifest faith:

   1. He heard the word.
   2. He placed his hope in the future according to that word.
   3. He refused to accept natural evidences that contradicted that word.
   4. He did not waiver in his commitment to that word.
   5. He rejoiced when the fulfillment of the word was realized.

   Scriptural faith is _____ , not the mind. It
   is in the present, not the future. It produces a positive change in the behavior and experience. It is based

   solely in God's Word and accepts the testimony of the senses _____
   when it agrees with the text of God's Word.

IV. HOW IS TRUE FAITH EXPRESSED IN THE LIFE OF THE BELIEVER?

There are two main ways in which faith is actively expressed in the life of the believer:

A. It is expressed by the _____ of the mouth (Romans 10:9; Matthew 10:32).

   ". . . For out of the abundance of the heart the mouth speaketh." Matthew 12:34

B. It is expressed by a life of _____ to the word received. Faith and works are inseparably linked (Romans 1:5; 15:18; 16:25, 26; James 2:14-26).

   "Even so faith, if it hath not works, is dead, being alone. Yea, a man may say, Thou hast faith, and I have works: shew me thy faith without thy works, and I will shew thee my faith by my works." James 2:17,18

V. HOW DO WE APPROPRIATE FAITH IN SPECIFIC SITUATIONS?

A. Locate the _____ in God's Word that fits the need (Philippians 4:19).

"For all the promises of God in him are yea, and in him Amen, unto the glory of God by us." II Corinthians 1:20

B. Fulfill all the _____ attached to that need (Deuteronomy 28:1, 2, 15).

"Commit thy way unto the Lord; trust also in Him; and He shall bring it to pass." Psalm 37:5

C. With patience accept the trying of your faith and God's testing of your faith through time of

_____ (Hebrews 6:12-15; Psalm 105:19).

"Knowing this, that the trying of your faith worketh patience. But let patience have her perfect work, that ye may be perfect and entire, wanting nothing." James 1:3-4

VI. WHAT CAN ONE DO TO INCREASE IN FAITH?

A. Settle in your hearts that God's Word is _____ (James 1:6, 7; II Peter 1:19; Psalm 18:30).

B. Put yourself in the place of _____ the Word of God (Romans 10:17; Galatians 3:2, 5).

C. Be hearers and _____ of the Word, not hearers only (Luke 8:15).

D. _____ the faith that you have (Matthew 9:20, 22; 14:25-29). Even in the physical body as we exercise our muscles, they increase.

E. _____ natural reasonings and philosophies of man that speak contrary to the clearly revealed Word of God (I Timothy 1:4-7; 6:20, 21; II Timothy 2:16-18; Romans 14:1; Colossians 2:8).

Conclusion: Faith toward God is simply to trust God, to have confidence in Him and His Word, to believe what God has said, that His Word is true and what He has promised He will perform. GOD makes a promise, FAITH believes it, HOPE anticipates it and PATIENCE quietly awaits it. The life of every believer in Christ is to be lived completely in this context. Faith must be the motivating factor for all that we do.

Water Baptism

Purpose: The purpose of this lesson is to bring us to an understanding that water baptism is the first step of obedience for the new believer and symbolizes a washing away of former sins and an identification with the death, burial and resurrection of the Lord Jesus Christ. This step is an essential part of the proper Christian birth.

Key Verse: "In whom also ye are circumcised with the circumcision made without hands, in putting off the body of the sins of the flesh by the circumcision of Christ: buried with Him in baptism, wherein also ye are risen with Him through the faith of the operation of God, who hath raised Him from the dead." Colossians 2:11, 12 KJV

I. WHAT IS THE MEANING OF THE WORD "BAPTIZE"?

The English word "baptize" is transliterated from a Greek word, "baptizo", which simply means "to dip, to overwhelm, to plunge, to submerge." It actually means "to cause something to be dipped or

_____ beneath the surface of water or some other fluid."

If this word was truly translated, rather than transliterated, the command in the New Testament would read, "Go ye therefore and teach all nations, immersing them in the name of the Father, and of the Son, and of the Holy Ghost." Matthew 28:19

II. WHY IS THE BELIEVER TO BE BAPTIZED?

A. Because Jesus commanded that believers be baptized (Mark 16:16; Matthew 28:19).

"If ye love me, keep my commandments." John 14:15

B. Because the apostles commanded it (Acts 2:37-39; 10:44-48).

C. Because Jesus was baptized to fulfill all righteousness (Matthew 3:13-17).

D. Because we validate our faith by our obedience to the Word of God (James 2:17, 18).

Water baptism is an essential part of obedience; it is not optional. To refuse water baptism is to live in disobedience to the revealed Word of God.

III. *WHAT ARE THE PREREQUISITES FOR WATER BAPTISM.*

Baptism in and of itself cannot save anyone. It is faith in the Lord Jesus Christ as one's Saviour that brings an individual to salvation. Therefore, baptism is only effectual for those who meet certain requirements. Those receiving baptism must have already laid the first two foundation stones in the Christian experience, namely:

A. _____ (Acts 2:38). This means one is not baptized merely because he wants to become part of a church group.

B. _____ (Acts 8:12; 10:47). This means that one must be old enough to know what they are doing.

"He that believeth and is baptized shall be saved."   Mark 16:16

IV. *WHAT TAKES PLACE IN WATER BAPTISM?*

We are baptized simply because it is commanded by God to do so. However, as we respond to the Word of the Lord in faith, some very important things will take place. Every person who goes into the waters of baptism should expect to experience the following, by faith:

A. To be _____ with the Lord Jesus Christ in His death, burial and resurrection (Romans 6:3-5, 11; Colossians 2:12; 3:1).

In baptism, the old man is crucified. In immersion, the old man is buried. But in rising out of the water,

the new man rises to walk in _____ of life.

"Therefore we are buried with him by baptism into death: that like as Christ was raised up from the dead by the glory of the Father, even so we also should walk in newness of life." Romans 6:4

B. A new _____ over life-dominating sins (Romans 6:11-18).

C. A spiritual _____ and renewal (Acts 22:16). The water itself affects no cleansing, but as we respond in faith to the commands of Christ the Holy Spirit works in connection with the God-ordained means.

D. An identification with _____ of the Lord (Acts 2:38; 8:12, 16; 10:48).

Kenyon puts it this way, "Baptism in this sense is equivalent to marriage. When the wife puts on marriage she takes her husband's name and enters into her husband's possessions and has legal right to her husband's home. When the believer is baptized into the name of Christ, he puts on all that is in Christ. He not only puts on the name, but takes his legal rights and privileges in Christ."

E. A circumcision of the _____ (Colossians 2:11, 12).

V. WHAT IS THE SIGNIFICANCE OF CIRCUMCISION OF THE HEART IN CONNECTION WITH WATER BAPTISM?

In the Old Testament, God gave a covenant to Abraham in which He required those who were participating in the covenant to accept and experience the sign and seal of the covenant which was a natural circumcision of the flesh (Genesis 17:10-14). In the New Testament, God has taken that seal and made it a spiritual requirement. In water baptism, we receive the spiritual experience of circumcision of the heart to which the natural rite pointed. The natural rite consisted of four elements that are all symbolic of something that takes place in the circumcision of the heart:

A. The cutting away of flesh. In baptism we _____ the old man (Colossians 2:11).

B. The shedding of blood. In baptism a death to _____ is to take place (Romans 6:3).

C. The eighth day. Natural circumcision took place on the eighth day, which is symbolic of new beginning

and resurrection life (I Peter 3:20, 21). In baptism we experience _____ and newness of life.

D. The new name given. In baptism we have _____ invoked over us: the name of the Lord Jesus Christ, the fulness of the Godhead bodily.

VI. HOW SHOULD WE BE BAPTIZED?

A. Scriptural baptism is baptism by _____ (See Question I).

B. Baptism is to be administered in _____ of the Lord Jesus Christ.

Jesus commanded that baptism was to be administered in the name of the Father and of the Son and of the Holy Ghost (Matt. 28:19, 20), which name the disciples came to see, on the basis of Jesus' ascension and exaltation (Acts 2:33-36), was the Lord Jesus Christ. When they baptized, they baptized in this manner (Acts 2:36-41; 8:12-16; 35-38; 10:48).

VII. WHAT IS THE RESPONSIBILITY OF THE BAPTIZED?

Even as the waters of the Red Sea served as a separation between the Egyptian life of slavery and the land of God's provision for the Israelites of old, so the waters of baptism should serve as a permanent landmark in the life of the believer. Baptism should signal three things:

A. _____ to the old way of life. This means a willingness to sever all connections with ungodliness and those who live in ungodliness.

B. _____ of living. This means that from baptism on, there will be a determination to live by the principles of God's kingdom.

C. _____ of Jesus. This means that the person who is baptized should see himself as a follower, a student and a witness to others of all that Jesus stands for.

Conclusion: It is very obvious that baptism is more than just an external experience in the Christian life. God wants to do something lasting and permanent at this special time. Sad to say, many people go down into the waters of baptism dry and come up wet and that is the extent of their experience. But if each individual would respond in faith to all that God says is available in baptism, baptism will be one of the greatest experiences of their Christian walk.

5

The Holy Spirit Baptism

Purpose: The purpose of this lesson is to further equip the believer in Christ not only by teaching them concerning the truth of the baptism of the Holy Spirit as an experience subsequent to and distinct from salvation, but by leading them into a personal experience of the endument with power from on high.

Key Verse: "But ye shall receive power, after that the Holy Ghost is come upon you: and ye shall be witnesses unto me both in Jerusalem, and in all Judea, and in Samaria, and unto the uttermost part of the earth." Acts 1:8 KJV

I. WHAT WAS THE RELATIONSHIP OF THE OLD TESTAMENT BELIEVERS TO THE WORK AND MINISTRY OF THE HOLY SPIRIT?

A. The Spirit came upon various men in Old Testament times that enabled them to do special feats of strength (Judges 11:29).

B. The Spirit of the Lord rested upon men (Numbers 11:25).

C. Men were filled with the Spirit in a temporary fashion to perform certain God-ordained tasks (Exodus 31:3).

In Old Testament times the Holy Spirit seemed to come upon and then withdraw from certain individuals as the need arose (I Samuel 10:6, 10; 16:14). One of the signs of the Messiah would be one on whom the Holy Spirit would remain (John 1:33).

II. HOW IS THE MINISTRY OF THE HOLY SPIRIT SEEN IN THE LIFE OF THE LORD JESUS, THE HEAD OF THE CHURCH?

It is important to see how the Holy Spirit moved in the life of Christ, for Christ is a pattern of that which is to flow into the Church which is His Body (Ephesians 1:22, 23).

A. CHRIST WAS:

Born of the Spirit (Luke 1:35)
Filled with Spirit (John 3:34)
Baptized with Spirit (Matthew 3:16, 17)
Led of the Spirit (Matthew 4:1)
Sealed by Spirit (John 6:27)
Empowered by Spirit (Luke 4:14)
Anointed by Spirit (Acts 10:38)

B. THE CHURCH IS TO BE:

Born of Spirit (John 3:5)
Filled with Spirit (Ephesians 3:19)
Baptized with Spirit (Acts 1:5)
Led of Spirit (Romans 8:14)
Sealed by Spirit (Ephesians 1:13)
Empowered by Spirit (Acts 1:8)
Anointed by Spirit (I John 2:27)

III. IS THE "BAPTISM OF THE HOLY SPIRIT" A SCRIPTURAL TERM?

_____ . It was used by John the Baptist (John 1:33), by Jesus (Acts 1:5) and by Peter (Acts 11:16).

IV. WHAT IS THE RELATIONSHIP OF CHRIST TO THE BAPTISM OF THE HOLY SPIRIT?

A. Jesus was baptized in the Holy Spirit after His water baptism in the Jordan (Matthew 3:16, 17; John 1:19-34). The Spirit came and remained on Him.

B. Part of Jesus' ministry is to baptize with the Holy Spirit (John 1:33). To make this clear, Jesus did not personally baptize anyone with water (John 4:2).

C. Jesus prophesied that this would be a believer's experience given on the basis of His exaltation and glorification (John 7:38, 39).

D. Jesus received this provision for the Church from the Father when He ascended into heaven (Acts 2:33).

V. WHAT IS THE BAPTISM OF THE HOLY SPIRIT?

A. It is the _____ of the Father (Acts 1:4,5; 2:33, 39).

B. It is the enduing with _____ to do the commands of Christ (Acts 1:8; Luke 24:49).

C. It is a _____ experience of which we can know that we have or have not received (Acts 19:2).

D. It is an operation of the Spirit distinct from and _____ the conversion experience (Acts 8:12, 15, 16).

E. It is something to be experienced as part of the Christian _____

_____ (Acts 2:38, 39).

VI. WHAT IS THE INITIAL EVIDENCE OF RECEIVING THE BAPTISM OF THE SPIRIT?

The only way to arrive at a conclusive answer to this question is by examining every case where individuals or groups of people received this experience in the New Testament.

A. On the day of Pentecost, the waiting disciples were all "filled with the Holy Ghost, and began to speak

with other _____ as the spirit gave them utterance." (Acts 2:4)

B. In Samaria, when Peter and John laid hands on those who were converted under Lhillip's ministry, we are told that "Simon saw that through laying on of the apostles' hands the Holy Ghost was given . . ." (Acts 8:18). Evidently, there was a visible sign that Simon saw, which is alluded to in Verse 21 when

Peter informed Simon that he did not have "part nor lot in this matter (lit. _____

_____).

C. The Gentiles experienced an outpouring of the Spirit after Peter's sermon at the house of Cornelius and

everyone present knew it "for they heard them speak with _____

_____ and magnify God" (Acts 10:44-46).

D. The disciples that Paul encountered in Ephesus "spake with _____

_____ , and prophesied (Acts 19:1-6) when Paul laid hands on them.

In every case where we have people experiencing the Baptism of the Spirit, we find a common denominator.

There was an immediate evidence of " _____

_____ ."

Ernest Gentile puts it this way, "The Bible does not say that you MUST speak in tongues to have the Baptism of the Holy Spirit, but it does teach us by illustration that if you have the Baptism of the Holy Spirit, you will be given the immediate evidence of speaking in tongues."

VII. WHO MAY RECEIVE THE BAPTISM OF THE HOLY SPIRIT?

_____ in Christ of all ages are candidates for the Baptism of the Holy Spirit (Mark 16:17). "For the promise is unto you, and to your children, and to all that are afar off, even as many as the Lord our God shall call" (Acts 2:38, 39).

For those who believe on Christ, the actual reception of the Spirit baptism is sometimes conditioned on the believer's knowing that there is such an experience available to them and that it is for now (Acts 19:1-6).

VIII. HOW DOES ONE RECEIVE THE BAPTISM OF THE HOLY SPIRIT?

We do not heceive the gifts of God by the works of the flesh (Galatians 3:2). All the gifts of God are of grace and are to be received by faith (Eph. 2:8-10). There are, however, several things that will help us to release our faith in this area:

A. Fulfill the prerequisites of repentance and faith _____
asking for this experience.

B. _____ , the baptizer with the Holy Spirit, to give you this gift (Matthew 3:11; Luke 11:9-13).

"I indeed baptize you with water unto repentance: but he that cometh after me is mightier than I, whose shoes I am not worthy to bear: he shall baptize you with the Holy Ghost, and with fire." (Matthew 3:11)

C. Yield your "unruly member" as an instrument of righteousness, _____

_____ that God will give you something other than what you desire.

D. Exercise your faith by _____ in an unknown language unto the Lord.

E. Once you have received the gift of the Holy Ghost, use your tongue _____

_____ as it is a key to spiritual vitality (Jude 20; I Corinthians 14:15, 18).

IX. WHAT ARE SOME BIBLICAL REASONS FOR SPEAKING IN OTHER TONGUES?

A. It is one of the signs of the believer (Mark 16:17).

B. It is a way for our spirit to be built up in faith (I Corinthians 14:4).

C. It is a way to magnify the Lord (Acts 10:46).

D. It is part of our spiritual armor (Ephesians 6:18).

E. It is spoken of as a refreshing (Isaiah 28:11, 12 with I Corinthians 14:21).

Conclusion: God wants every believer who is born of the Spirit to be baptized in the Spirit as well. The Baptism of the Holy Spirit is absolutely necessary in every Christian for the service that Christ demands and expects of us. Jesus and the Apostles all waited to enter into their ministry until this "endument with power" was experienced. Let us never see such a wonderful provision of God as an option, but let us seek and find (Matthew 7:7) and hunger and thirst (Matthew 5:6).

6

Christian Discipleship

Purpose: The purpose of this lesson is to help us to see that every Christian is also to be a disciple of Jesus, and that the Lord is not just interested in the salvation of the spirit of man, but also in sanctification of the mind, will and emotions of man. This will take place as believers come under the authority of Christ in their lives.

Key Verse: "... Whosoever will come after me, let him deny himself, and take up his cross, and follow me. For whosoever will save his life shall lose it; but whosoever shall lose his life for my sake and the Gospel's, the same shall save it." Mark 8:34-35 KJV

I. WHAT IS JESUS' COMMAND CONCERNING DISCIPLESHIP?

When Jesus commissioned His disciples after the resurrection, He gave them a fourfold charge:

A. _____ . "Go ye into all the world, and preach the gospel to every creature." (Mark 16:15)

B. _____ . "Go ye therefore, and teach (lit. make disciples) all nations, baptizing them in the name of the Father, and of the Son, and of the Holy Ghost: teaching them to observe all things whatsoever I have commanded you." (Matthew 28:19-20)

C. _____ . "But ye shall receive power, after that the Holy Ghost is come upon you: and ye shall be witnesses unto me ..." (Acts 1:8)

D. _____ . "Jesus saith unto him, Feed my sheep." (John 21:17)

These four things must be experienced in this order in the life of every believer.

II. WHAT IS A DISCIPLE?

A. The word "disciple" is used over 250 times in the New Testament and simply means:

  1. A _____ or _____ one.
  2. A learner or pupil.
  3. One who accepts or receives instruction or doctrines of another.
  4. A disciplined one.

B. The word "discipline", which is closely related, means:

  1. Training that develops self-control or character.
  2. Submission to control.

  3. _____ .
  4. Treatment that corrects or adjusts.

III. WHAT DOES IT MEAN TO BE A DISCIPLE OF JESUS CHRIST?

A. It means that we are willing to treat Him as our _____ and master (Matthew 10:24).

B. It means that we are willing to be _____ and instructed in His ways (Matthew 5:1-2).

C. It means that we must be willing to _____ to His commands (Luke 6:46; Matthew 7:21).

D. It means that we must be willing to be _____ and adjusted by the Word of the Lord (Proverbs 3:11-12; Hebrews 12:5-13).

IV. WHAT DOES IT COST TO BE A DISCIPLE OF JESUS CHRIST?

We are clearly instructed in the Word of God that before we begin building, we should count the cost (Luke 14:25-33). Salvation is a free gift from God. We can do nothing to earn it or deserve it (Ephesians 2:8-9), but if we are to respond to that call of discipleship, it will cost us everything that we have (Luke 5:11).

"He that loveth father or mother more than me is not worthy of me: and he that loveth son or daughter more than me is not worthy of me. And he that taketh not his cross, and followeth after me, is not worthy of me." (Matthew 10:37-38).

This means that everything in our life has to take second place to our relationship to the Lord, including:

A. Our _____ (Matthew 8:19, 20; Luke 9:58).

B. Our _____ and relatives (Matthew 10:37-38).

C. Our _____ (Matthew 4:18-22).

D. Our _____ (Matthew 19:16-22).

This does not mean that the Lord will demand these things of us, but it does mean that we would _____ _____ to offer them up if He did (Matthew 16:24-26).

V. WHAT IS THE REWARD OF THE LIFE OF DISCIPLESHIP?

The only reason we can become such a disciple to the Lord Jesus Christ is because He only has our best interest in mind. The Lord never asks us to give something up unless He plans to give us something

_____ in return.

"And Jesus answered and said, Verily I say unto you, There is no man that hath left house, or brethren, or sisters, or father, or mother, or wife, or children, or lands, for my sake, and the gospel's, but he shall receive an hundredfold now in this time, houses, and brethren, and sisters, and mothers, and children, and lands, with persecutions; and in the world to come eternal life." Mark 10:29-30

"I am come that they might have life, and that they might have it more abundantly." John 10:10

VI. WHAT IS THE GOAL OF THE LIFE OF DISCIPLESHIP?

There are several goals that will be achieved for those who become disciples:

A. To be a _____ , mature Christian able to weather the storms of life (Ephesians 4:13-14).

B. To be a true reflection of _____ to the world (Eph. 4:13; Acts 11:26).

C. To be the kind of Christian that others can _____ and pattern their lives after (I Corinthians 11:1; Titus 2:7-8).

D. To be the kind of Christian that God can use to _____ to others (John 15:8, 12-17).

E. To receive ultimately from the Lord the commendation of a _____

_____ servant (Matthew 25:21).

"Wherefore the rather, brethren, give diligence to make your calling and election sure: for if you do these things, ye shall never fall: for so an entrance shall be ministered unto you abundantly into the everlasting kingdom of our Lord and Saviour Jesus Christ." II Peter 1:10-11

Conclusion: The life of discipleship is really not an option for those who want to reach the above goals in their life. Unfortunately, many believers live a life far below God's standard for them and, hence, never fully experience the great rewards and blessings that come from a life of total surrender to the King of Kings and Lord of Lords. As believers, we must be willing to accept the challenge of discipleship if we are to prove ". . . what is that good, and acceptable, and perfect, will of God" (Romans 12:1-2).

7

Fellowship

Purpose: The purpose of this lesson is to demonstrate to the believer that God never intended for His people to live in isolation or separated from each other, but that in His purpose He intended that they be rightly related to one another in unity, flowing together as a harmonious whole, to carry on a corporate ministry to the world.

Key Verse: "I therefore, the prisoner of the Lord, beseech you that ye walk worthy of the vocation wherewith ye are called, with all lowliness and meekness, with longsuffering, forbearing one another in love; endeavoring to keep the unity of the spirit in the bond of peace. There is one body, and one spirit, even as ye are called in one hope of your calling; one Lord, one faith, one baptism, one God and Father of all, who is above all, and through all, and in you all." Ephesians 4:1-6 KJV

I. WHAT DOES THE WORD "FELLOWSHIP" MEAN?

A. The actual meaning of the Greek word, translated "fellowship" in the New Testament, is

" _____ ".

It means to be a sharer, or a partner in something.

B. In relation to the people of God it describes the partnership, _____

_____ or relationship that believers enter into by virtue of their common experience of salvation and mutual participation in the Body of Christ.

II. WHAT ARE THE TWO ASPECTS OF CHRISTIAN FELLOWSHIP?

Fellowship for the believer is seen in _____ : vertically and horizontally.

''That which we have seen and heard declare we unto you, that ye also may have fellowship with us: and truly our fellowship is with the Father, and with his Son Jesus Christ.'' I John 1:3

A. Vertical fellowship is fellowship _____ . Fellowship with God is the foundation for all other Christian fellowship. Fellowship with God is established when we lay down our will and accept God's authority in our lives on the basis of the death, burial and resurrection of our Lord Jesus Christ (I Corinthians 1:9; Ephesians 2:12-18).

This fellowship is cultivated in prayer, praise and worship in Spirit and in truth (John 4:23-24).

B. Horizontal fellowship is fellowship _____ . Once fellowship with God has been established, we can have proper fellowship with one another. When God is truly our first love and our desire is to please Him, then the way is open for the Lord to break down all barriers that separate us from one another.

This fellowship is cultivated in our inter-relating one with another in the Body of Christ (Acts 2:42).

III. *WHAT ARE SOME OF THE WAYS CHRISTIAN FELLOWSHIP IS EXPRESSED?*

Christian fellowship is expressed in spiritual ways, as well as in practical ways.

A. Some spiritual avenues of fellowship include:

1. Praying one for another (James 5:16)
2. Exhorting one another (Hebrews 3:13; 10:25).
3. Edifying one another (Romans 14:19)
4. Bearing one another's burdens (Galatians 6:2, 5)
5. Singing, praising and worshipping together (Colossians 3:16)
6. Comforting one another (I Thessalonians 4:18)
7. Forgiving one another (Ephesians 4:32)

B. Some practical avenues of fellowship include:

1. Receiving one another into friendship (Romans 15:7)
2. Serving one another in practical ways (Galatians 5:13)
3. House-to-house fellowship (Acts 2:46)
4. Showing hospitality to those in need (Romans 12:13)
5. Being considerate one of another (Ephesians 4:32)
6. Helping the needy financially (I John 3:16-18)
7. Getting to know and appreciate each other.

''A new commandment I give unto you, that ye love one another; as I have loved you, that ye also love one

another. By this _____
that ye are my disciples, if ye have love one to another.'' John 13:34-35

IV. *WITH WHAT ARE WE FORBIDDEN TO FELLOWSHIP?*

When we enter into the Kingdom of God there should be an immediate _____

_____ from certain things that are totally inconsistent with the Christian lifestyle.

A. The unregenerate world (Ephesians 5:11; Psalm 94:20)
B. Satanic spirits and cults (I Corinthians 10:20)
C. Unrighteousness (II Corinthians 6:14)
D. False religion (II Peter 2; Jude 4)
E. False doctrine (II John 1:9-11; Galatians 1:7-10)

V. WHAT LIMITATIONS DOES GOD PLACE ON OUR FELLOWSHIP WITH OTHERS WHO PROFESS TO BE BELIEVERS?

While we are to endeavor to maintain the unity of the Spirit in the bond of peace until we all come to the unity of the faith (Ephesians 4:2, 13), there are limitations that God places on our fellowship even with others who profess to be Christian. These limitations include both areas of doctrine and practice.

A. _____ . Any doctrine which attacks the fundamental steps of the process of redemption should not be fellowshipped. This would include such things as the deity of Christ, the virgin birth, the humanity of Christ, the physical death, burial and resurrection of Christ, the depravity of man outside of Christ and the power of the blood of Christ to cleanse from sin (Titus 3:10; Romans 16:17).

B. _____ . Those who claim to be Christians, but who live in a way that is a reproach to His name, are not to be fellowshipped (Matthew 18:15-17; I John 1:7; 2:10-11; II Thessalonians 3:6). These things include:

1. Coveteous — Inordinately desirous or greedy.
2. Idolatrous — Inordinately fond of a person or things above the Lord.
3. Railer — Abusive and scornful language.
4. Drunkenness — Habitually drinking to excess.
5. Extortion — Obtaining gain by dishonest means.
6. Fornication — Illicit sexual relationships.
7. Hardness of Heart — Refusing to reconcile an offense with a brother.

With individuals who fall into these categories we are instructed "do not _____

_____ with them" and "do not _____

_____ with them" (I Corinthians 5:11; II Thessalonians 3:14).

Conclusion: God is very much concerned that all who belong to Him live in proper relationship to Him and to each other in His Body. This is why, in the New Testament, those who were added to the Lord (Acts 5:14) were also added to the Church (Acts 2:41, 47). When we were saved we became part of a great family — the family of God! God is our Father and all those who know Him are our brothers and sisters. God is very concerned that His children love and accept one another and are united to do His work. God has a beautiful work for His family here on earth to do and a structure to follow and be a part of while doing it.

8

RESTORING THE CHURCH — PRINCIPLES OF CHURCH LIFE

Communion

Purpose: The purpose of this lesson is to help us to understand the importance of communion as one of the main ordinances of the church and to grow in our appreciation of what is available to every Christian at the "Table of the Lord".

Key Verse: "For I have received of the Lord that which also I delivered unto you, that the Lord Jesus the same night in which He was betrayed took bread: and when He had given thanks, He brake it, and said, take, eat: this is my body, which is broken for you: this do in remembrance of me. After the same manner also He took the cup, when He had supped, saying, this cup is the New Testament in my blood: this do ye, as oft as ye drink it, in remembrance of me. For as often as ye eat this bread, and drink this cup, ye do shew the Lord's death till He come." I Corinthians 11:23-26 KJV

I. WHAT ARE SOME OF THE NAMES AND TITLES THAT ARE HISTORICALLY GIVEN TO THIS ORDINANCE?

There are many names and titles that are associated with this ordinance; some of them are Biblical, some historical, some traditional. All of them have an element of truth to them.

A. The Lord's _____ (I Corinthians 11:20). It is referred to in this way because it was at Christ's last supper with the disciples, prior to his crucifixion, that Jesus established this ordinance (Matthew 26:26-29) and it points to a future supper that all believers of all ages will once again eat with Christ (Revelation 19:9, 17).

B. The Lord's _____ or the _____ of the Lord (I Corinthians 10:21). A table speaks to us of a place of feasting, love and fellowship. The Lord has provided a place for us to sup with Him in an intimate way.

C. The _____ (I Corinthians 10:16). The word "communion" means an intimate sharing of one person to another. Communion is to be a time of intimacy with the Lord and His Body.

D. Breaking _____ (Acts 20:7). This title refers back to when Jesus initiated communion and he took the bread, broke it and blessed it (Matthew 26:26).

"And upon the first day of the week, when the disciples came together to break bread . . ." Acts 20:7

E. Other non-biblical terms:

1. Eucharist. This word comes from the Greek word which means "giving thanks" (I Corinthians 14:16). Certainly, as we remember the Lord, thanksgiving should fill our hearts.

2. Sacrament. This word comes from a Latin word meaning "holy" or "set apart". The Communion Table should certainly be hallowed and reverenced by all.

II. WHAT IS THE FOUNDATION FOR THIS ORDINANCE IN THE BIBLE?

A. From the first chapters (Genesis 3:8) to the last chapters (Revelation 21:1-3) of the Bible, God has revealed Himself as one who delights in and desires to have intimate fellowship and relationship with His creation.

B. Even though sin separated man from God, God has always provided a means whereby this intimate relationship could be experienced in His house.

"And let them make me a sanctuary; that I may dwell among them." Exodus 25:8

C. In the Old Testament, at different times, God provided different avenues through which this desire could be manifest.

1. The Altar of Sacrifice (Exodus 20:24).

2. The Table of Shewbread (Leviticus 24:5-9).

D. Under the New Covenant, the table of the Lord's presence is the Communion Table.

III. WHAT SYMBOLS DID JESUS USE IN ESTABLISHING THE COMMUNION?

A. Bread (Luke 22:19).

1. The Bread speaks of the body of Christ broken for sinful man.

2. The Bread which Jesus provided is necessary for spiritual life (John 6:58).

B. Fruit of the Vine (Matthew 26:29).

1. The Fruit of the Vine speaks of the blood of Christ that was shed for sinful man for cleansing sin (Matthew 26:28).

2. Only the Blood of Christ has the power to cleanse from sin (I John 1:7).

IV. WHAT SPIRITUAL REALITIES ARE DEMONSTRATED AND EXPERIENCED AT THE LORD'S TABLE?

Everything that we experience in the Christian life we experience as we exercise faith in the Word of God. Going through a certain formality effects nothing. However, as we exercise faith in the Word of God we should expect communion to be a very meaningful time.

A. It should be a time of _____ (I Corinthians 11:24-25). As Christians, we should continually remember the death, burial and resurrection of Christ and what it provided for us.

B. It should be a time of _____ (I Corinthians 10:16). All believers need to renew and maintain a communion relationship with the Lord.

C. It should be a time of _____ (I Corinthians 10:17). At the Table believers should be united around the Lord and recognize their interdependence and need for the spiritual Body of Christ.

D. It should be a time of _____ (Luke 22:15). Christ's death was the highest expression of His love for us. The Table of the Lord is a feast of His love.

E. It should be a time of _____ (I Corinthians 11:29-30). The truths found at the Table of the Lord should have healing effects on relationships among believers and bring health to the physical body.

F. It should be a time of _____ (I Corinthians 11:28-32). Every believer should examine his heart to make sure it is free from enmity toward God and enmity toward our fellowman (Luke 22:21; I Corinthians 11:29).

G. It should be a time of _____ (Matthew 26:27). As we remember Christ's work, a new spirit of thanksgiving should be ours.

H. It should be a time of _____ (I Corinthians 10:16). God's desire is to bless His people through the blessed bread and the blessed cup.

I. It should be a time of _____ (I Corinthians 11:26). Up to the Second Coming of Christ the practice of communion in the Church is a visible sign and witness to the death of Christ.

V. HOW CAN A SINFUL MAN FIND A PLACE AT THE KING'S TABLE?

It is only on the basis of God's infinite love, mercy and grace that we can sit and feast at the Table of the Lord. Gratitude should fill our hearts every time we share this meal together. The magnitude of Christ's love is depicted in the Old Testament account of Mephibosheth finding a place at the Table of the king (II Samuel 9:1-13).

Conclusion: Paul the Apostle had a great love and appreciation for the Table of the Lord. His understanding did not come because he was familiar with the procedure, because he read about it in a book or because he was told by a church leader. Paul's understanding came to him by a personal revelation by the Spirit of God (I Corinthians 11:23). As you read and meditate on the Scriptures in this lesson, ask God to give you a personal revelation of the love of God expressed to you in the Table of the Lord.

Study Questions

Lessons 1-8

LESSON 1 — WHY STUDY DOCTRINE?

1. The word "doctrine" means _____ .

2. In order for doctrine to be effective in our lives it must meet five requirements.

   It must be (1) _____ (2) _____

   (3) _____ (4) _____

   and (5) _____ .

LESSON 2 — REPENTANCE FROM DEAD WORKS

3. The root meaning of the word "repentance" is _____

   _____ .

4. The fruits of repentance are evidenced in (1) _____

   (2) _____ (3) _____

   (4) _____ (5) _____

   and (6) _____ .

LESSON 3 — FAITH TOWARD GOD

5. The only source of true biblical faith is _____ .

6. Scriptural faith is based solely on God's Word and accepts the testimony of the senses only when _____

_____ .

LESSON 4 — WATER BAPTISM

7. The word "baptize" means _____ .

8. Five things that take place in baptism include (1) _____

_____ (2) _____ (3) _____

(4) _____ (5) _____ .

LESSON 5 — HOLY SPIRIT BAPTISM

9. The evidence in the book of Acts of receiving the Baptism of the Holy Spirit was _____

_____ .

10. Three biblical reasons for speaking in tongues include (1) _____

_____ (2) _____

(3) _____ .

LESSON 6 — CHRISTIAN DISCIPLINE

11. Jesus gave the fourfold charge to his disciples to (1) _____

_____ (2) _____

(3) _____ (4) _____ .

12. Salvation is a free gift from God and we can do nothing to earn it or deserve it; but, if we are to respond

to the call of discipleship, it will cost _____

_____ .

LESSON 7 — FELLOWSHIP

13. Fellowship for the believer is seen in two directions (1) _____

_____ and (2) _____ .

14. Those who claim to be Christians, but who live in a way that is _____

_____ are not to be fellowshipped.

LESSON 8 — COMMUNION

15. The foundation for this ordinance in the Bible is God's desire to have _____

    _____ .

16. It is only on the basis of God's _____

    _____ that we can sit and feast at the Table of the Lord.

Prayer and Fasting

Purpose: The purpose of this lesson is to develop an understanding of the basic Christian disciplines of prayer and fasting, to help believers to see the importance of these disciplines and to challenge the believers in regard to the regular and systematic practices of these disciplines in their lives.

Key Verse: "Then shall ye call upon me, and ye shall go and pray unto me, and I will hearken unto you. And ye shall seek me, and find me, when ye shall search for me with all your heart. And I will be found of you, saith the Lord: . . ." Jeremiah 29:12-14a KJV

I. WHAT IS PRAYER?

A. Prayer is spending time in conversation with God.

B. Prayer is the act of beseeching God earnestly for someone or something.

C. Prayer involves communion with God and a recognition of His presence.

II. WHAT IS FASTING?

A. Fasting involves denying the body natural food and drink that we may intensify our sensitivity and openness to the Lord.

B. Fasting is a time of placing the desires of the flesh under the desires of the spirit, or, as it is sometimes called, "chastening of the soul" (Psalms 69:10, 11).

C. Fasting was a regular practice of the Early Church.

    1. It was practiced individually (II Corinthians 11:27).

    2. It was practiced corporately (Acts 13:2).

III. WHO PROVIDES THE GREATEST EXAMPLE OF PRAYER AND FASTING?

Jesus. Jesus Christ, who was the only perfect man, gave us a perfect example of communion with the Heavenly Father and, in doing so, demonstrated His absolute dependence on the Father (Luke 3:21; 4:1, 2; 5:16; 6:12; 9:18; 11:1).

"And in the morning, rising up a great while before day, he went out, and departed into a solitary place, and there prayed." Mark 1:35 KJV

IV. WHAT ATTITUDES SHOULD BE INVOLVED IN PRAYER AND FASTING?

A. We should pray in _____ (Hebrews 11:6).

B. We should come _____ before the Lord (Psalms 35:13).

C. We should come desiring God's _____ (I John 5:14-16).

D. We should come with _____ motivation (Psalms 24:3, 4; Isaiah 58:6, 7).

E. We should come without _____ (Matthew 6:5-18).

V. WHAT ARE SOME BIBLICAL GUIDELINES GOVERNING PRAYER?

A. Believers should have an attitude of prayer or open communion with God at _____ _____ times (I Thessalonians 5:17; Romans 1:9).

B. Believers should have a specific time set aside for _____ prayer (Psalms 5:1-3; 55:16,17).

C. Believers should spend time _____ to God in prayer times, realizing that prayer is two-way communication (Psalms 143:8; Isaiah 40:31).

VI. WHAT ARE DIFFERENT KINDS OF PRAYER FOUND IN THE BIBLE?

There are many kinds of prayer mentioned in the Bible. All the different forms are valid and are to be found operating at various times in the life of the believer.

A. Perservering, or Fervant, Prayer (James 5:16; Luke 11:5-13).

B. Intercessory Prayer (I Timothy 2:1).

C. Giving of Thanks (I Timothy 2:1; Philippians 4:6).

D. Prayer in the Spirit (I Corinthians 14:14).

E. Prayer and Fasting (Matthew 17:21).

F. Supplication (I Timothy 2:1, 2).

VII. IN WHAT REALMS SHOULD OUR PRAYER LIFE BE PRACTICED?

A. _____ . Much of our prayer life will be in secret on a daily basis (Matthew 6:5-7).

B. _____ . Often we will solicit the prayer support of others to see special needs met (Matthew 18:19, 20).

C. _____ . The whole church will also have a corporate life together in prayer (Acts 2:42; 4:24; 13:1-3).

    1. The House of the Lord is to be a house of prayer (Matthew 21:13).

    2. The House of the Lord is a place where the voices of God's people will be heard in prayer, praise and thanksgiving (Psalms 64:1; 66:19; 18:6).

VIII. IS PRAYER AND FASTING ONLY A RELIGIOUS FORMALITY?

No. Absolutely not! Prayer and fasting are much more than an external form. God promises to respond to our prayers (II Chronicles 7:14). Prayer definitely changes things (Psalms 91:14, 15).

"And this is the confidence that we have in him, that, if we ask any thing according to his will, he heareth us: And if we know that he hear us, whatsoever we ask, we know that we have the petitions that we desired of him." I John 5:14, 15 KJV

Conclusion: Prayer and fasting are not optional disciplines in the life of the believer. Every believer must make a place for these practices in their life in order to maintain and ever deepen their personal relationship to God. The corporate prayer life of the church is vital and necessary and should be entered into by all; but it is no substitute for the personal prayer life of the individual. God is willing to give us all the grace to lay these foundations properly in our life.

Christian Stewardship

Purpose: The purpose of this lesson is to demonstrate to the believer his responsibility to God in the use of his life so that he will be equipped to make decisions in life that are consistent with this knowledge.

Key Verse: "What? Know ye not that your body is the temple of the Holy Ghost which is in you, which ye have of God, and ye are not your own? For ye are bought with a price: therefore glorify God in your body, and in your spirit, which are God's." I Corinthians 6:19, 20 KJV

I. WHAT IS A STEWARD?

A. The dictionary defines a steward as "a person entrusted with the management of estates or affairs not his own; an administrator."

B. The New Testament word translated "steward" means "the manager of a household or household affairs; a manager" (I Corinthians 4:1, 2; I Peter 4:10).

C. A steward is an individual who has been delegated authority by an owner to oversee his possessions, property and household affairs.

D. Stewards were common in the Biblical culture. Most wealthy people and rulers had stewards to whom they entrusted the oversight of personnel and property.

    1. Abraham had Eliezer (Genesis 15:2). He proved to be very faithful (Genesis 24:1-9).

    2. Elisha had Gehazi (II Kings 4:12). He proved to be an unwise steward (II Kings 5:20-27).

II. HOW IS THE CONCEPT OF STEWARDSHIP SEEN IN THE BELIEVER'S RELATIONSHIP TO GOD?

A. God is the owner of all things (Genesis 14:19, 22; Psalms 24:1; 50:1-12; 68:19; 89:11; Haggai 2:8). As the owner of all things God is:

   1. The giver or source (James 1:17).

   2. The One to whom account is given (Romans 14:12).

   3. The rewarder (Hebrews 11:6).

B. The believer is a steward (Matthew 25:14-30; Luke 19:11-26). As a steward, the believer is:

   1. The receiver (I Corinthians 4:7).

   2. Accountable and responsible to the owner (Romans 14:12; Luke 16:2).

   3. The one rewarded for faithfulness (Matthew 25:21, 23).

III. *WHAT ARE THE DIFFERENT REALMS IN WHICH STEWARDSHIP IS TO BE RECOGNIZED AND PRACTICED?*

A. Stewardship involves, first of all and most importantly, a giving of one's _____

   _____ (I Corinthians 6:19, 20; Romans 12:1, 2; Acts 17:25).

B. Stewardship involves a wise and honorable use of one's _____
   (Psalms 90:12; Proverbs 24:30-34).

C. Stewardship involves a wise investment and cultivation of individual _____

   _____ (Matthew 25:14-30).

D. Stewardship involves a proper understanding and use of one's _____

   _____ (Matthew 6:19-21; Colossians 3:1, 2).

E. Stewardship involves a careful and purposeful use of all _____
   (I Corinthians 16:1, 2).

IV. *WHAT IS A DEFINITION OF CHRISTIAN STEWARDSHIP?*

Stewardship is the practice of systematic and proportionate giving of time, abilities and material possessions based on the conviction that these are a trust from God to be used in His service for the benefit of His Kingdom. It is a divine/human partnership, with God as the senior partner. It is a way of living; the recognition of God's ownership of one's person, powers and possessions and the faithful use of these for the advancement of Christ's Kingdom in this world.

V. *WHAT ARE THE PRIMARY QUALITIES OF A GOOD STEWARD?*

A. Faithfulness and loyalty (I Corinthians 4:1, 2; Matthew 21:40, 41).

B. Industriousness (Matthew 25:26; Romans 12:11).

C. Discipline and obedience (Colossians 3:22; Titus 2:9).

D. Fruitfulness and productivity (Matthew 25:20).

E. Humility and a servant's heart (I Corinthians 4:7).

VI. *WHAT TRUTHS DID JESUS EMPHASIZE IN HIS TEACHING ON STEWARD-SHIP?*

Jesus' main teaching on stewardship is found in two main parables in Matthew 25:14-30 and Luke 16:1-13. These accounts bring out the following truths:

A. If we do not use what God has given us we will _____ .

B. God expects us to use our talents to bring _____ to His Kingdom.

C. God expects us to use great _____ as we use our talents.

D. Even though God does not appear to be giving direct oversight to what we are doing, yet there is a day

of _____ .

E. The _____ will be rewarded by the Lord.

F. The wicked and _____ will be judged by the Lord.

G. _____ over natural, material things will qualify us for true spiritual riches.

VII. *WHAT KINDS OF QUESTIONS SHOULD A BELIEVER ASK HIMSELF IN THIS AREA OF STEWARDSHIP?*

A. Do I daily acknowledge that all I have belongs to God?

B. Do I seek God's approval above man's approval in the lifestyle I lead?

C. Do I use my time, talents, abilities and finances in a way that would bring glory to God?

D. Am I contributing to the extension of the Kingdom of God by the use of all that I have?

E. Am I managing the affairs of my life in such a way that it will be easy for God to say to me, "Well done, thou good and faithful servant"?

Conclusion: Christian stewardship describes the position and responsibility of the Christian to manage or administer as a steward for God the things which God has committed to him in this life. We are not our own. Jesus Christ has bought us at an infinite cost. We belong completely to Him. Everything we do in life should reflect this fact. Every person is endowed with a free will and can choose to return to God that which belongs to Him or he can withhold from Him that which is rightfully His. Let us all prove to be good stewards of the manifold grace of God (I Peter 4:10).

11

Stewardship of Finances

Purpose: The purpose of this lesson is to demonstrate that every believer is accountable to God in the area of personal finances and that God's way to financial prosperity and blessing is different and higher than man's way of success.

Key Verse: "But this I say, he which soweth sparingly shall reap also sparingly; and he which soweth bountifully shall reap also bountifully. Every man according as he purposeth in his heart, so let him give; not grudgingly, or of necessity: for God loveth a cheerful giver. And God is able to make all grace abound towahd you; thst ye, always having all sufficiency in all things, may abound to every good work:" II Corinthians 9:6-8 KJV

I. IS IT SPIRITUAL TO TALK ABOUT MONEY?

Yes.

A. The Gospels contain more warnings concerning the misuse of money than any other singular subject. One in every four verses in Matthew, Mark and Luke deals with money.

B. One in every six verses in the whole of the New Testament makes some reference to money.

C. Almost one half of the parables of Jesus make reference to money and its misuse, particularly the area of coveteousness.

D . The only one of the twelve apostles to fall (Judas) fell over money (John 12:4-8; 13:27; Acts 1:25; Matthew 26:14-16; Jn. 12:4-6).

E. The first sin recorded in the early church concerned hypocrisy in the giving of money to the Lord (Acts 5:1-10).

F. Many a man in the Bible shipwrecked spiritually because of the improper use of or desire for money.

1. Balaam used his spiritual gift for personal gain (Numbers 22-24).

2. Achan brought judgment on all Israel when he yielded to coveteousness (Joshua 7).

3. Gehazi tried to take material advantage of another's ministry (II Kings 5).

II. WHAT WARNING DOES THE NEW TESTAMENT GIVE US CONCERNING MONEY?

The Bible clearly teaches us that money is not evil in and of itself. It is our love for money more than our love for God that will cause us to stumble in the area of coveteousness. For this reason the Bible gives strong warnings.

A. We are warned not to make the accumulation of wealth our main ambition in life (Luke 12:16-21; I Timothy 6:9).

B. We are warned not to value material gain above spiritual gain (I Timothy 6:6, 11).

C. We are warned that a love for money will end in destruction (I Timothy 6:9-11).

III. WHAT IS A "TITHE"?

A. The word "tithe" comes from a Hebrew word which means _____ .

A tithe of one's income (or increase), therefore, is one-tenth (ten percent). Tithing refers to the practice of systematically giving ten percent of one's income back to the Lord for His work.

B. Tithing was the common practice of holy men of God in Old Testament days.

1. Prior to the giving of the law, God's people tithed voluntarily.

   a. Abraham gave a tenth to Melchizedek (Genesis 14:18-20).

   b. Jacob gave a tenth at Bethel (Genesis 28:22).

2. When God gave the law to Moses, tithing was a major part of His overall financial system (Leviticus 27:30-33; Numbers 18:20-32).

3. Jesus confirmed tithing in His teaching and practice (Matthew 23:23; Luke 11:42; 18:12; Hebrews 7:1-21).

C. Tithing is to serve as a reminder that _____ comes from and belongs to the Lord (Deuteronomy 8:11, 17-18).

D. Tithing and giving is God's cure for _____ (Matthew 6:19-21; Ephesians 4:28).

E. Tithing is the _____ of our giving (Deuteronomy 12:6). Freewill offerings and giving to the poor should also be part of our giving (Galatians 2:10).

IV. WHAT ARE SOME MISCONCEPTIONS ABOUT TITHING?

There are many people who have unscriptural views of tithing.

A. Some say you can give money wherever you want. BUT God says there is a designated place (Deuteronomy 12:5, 6, 13, 14).

B. Some say that you can designate on your envelope where the tithe is to be used. BUT God says the tithe is to go for the service of His house (Numbers 18:21-24).

C. Some say that you can borrow your tithes and pay them back later. BUT God says if you do borrow them, when you pay them back, you must add a fifth more to the initial tithe (Leviticus 27:31).

D. Some say that God doesn't care *what* we give, only *how* we give. BUT God says that He is concerned with both (Mark 12:41-44; Matthew 5:20).

V. WHAT ARE SOME CLEAR NEW TESTAMENT PRINCIPLES THAT SHOULD GOVERN OUR GIVING?

The New Testament, in every case, elevates the Old Testament practices to a higher and more spiritual level. Rather than giving merely because we have to, there are other factors that New Testament believers need to consider.

As committed New Testament believers, we should:

A. Give _____ to the Lord first (II Corinthians 8:5).

B. Give _____ (II Corinthians 8:3, 12).

C. Give _____ (II Corinthians 9:7).

D. Give _____ , liberally (II Corinthians 8:2; 9:13).

E. Give _____ (II Corinthians 9:6; 8:14-15).

F. Give _____ (I Corinthians 16:1-2).

G. Give _____ (II Corinthians 9:7),

H. Give _____ (II Corinthians 8:24).

I. Give _____ (II Corinthians 9:11, 12).

J. Give _____ (Hebrews 13:16).

K. Give as a _____ to the Lord and His saints (II Corinthians 9:12, 13).

VI. WHAT ARE SIX SURPRISES THAT A TITHER CAN EXPECT TO FIND?

A systematic tither is going to be surprised

A. At the deepening of his spiritual life in paying the tithe.

B. At the ease in meeting obligations with nine-tenths.

C. At the amount of money that he has for the Lord's work.

D. At the ease in going from one-tenth to larger giving.

E. At the preparation that tithing gives to a faithful and wise steward over the remainder of his income.

F. At yourself for not adopting the plan sooner!

Conclusion: If a person does not give tithes, the Bible clearly teaches that this man is robbing God (Malachi 3:8-10). The tithe, in reality, does not belong to us; it belongs to God (Leviticus 27:30-33). But worse than that, if a person does not tithe, he is not putting himself in the place of divine blessing and prosperity. God indicates that if we put Him first in our giving, He will work for us in special ways, including restraining the devourer and opening special windows of blessing. May the Lord help us to overcome coveteousness and find a release in tithing.

"Will a man rob God? Yet ye have robbed me. But ye say, Wherein have we robbed thee? In tithes and offerings. Ye are cursed with a curse: for ye have robbed me, even this whole nation. Bring ye all the tithes into the storehouse, that there may be meat in mine house, and prove me now herewith, saith the Lord of hosts, if I will not open you the windows of heaven, and pour you out a blessing, that there shall not be room enough to receive it. And I will rebuke the devourer for your sakes, and he shall not destroy the fruits of your ground; neither shall your vine cast her fruit before the time in the field, saith the Lord of hosts." Malachi 3:8-11 KJV

12

Divine Healing

Purpose: The purpose of this lesson is to give us an appreciation for what God has provided for us in the atonement, to inspire faith in the heart of God's people to respond to Him as their healer, to remove doubts as to whether or not this provision is for the church today and to motivate the people of God to begin to look to the Lord with expectancy in the area of healing for the Body.

Key Verse: "Bless the Lord, O my soul, and forget not all His benefits: who forgiveth all thine iniquities; who healeth all thy diseases; who redeemeth thy life from destruction; who crowneth thee with lovingkindness and tender mercies . . ." Psalms 103:2-4 KJV

I. WHAT IS THE ORIGIN OF SICKNESS AND DISEASE?

A. Sickness was unknown on the earth until man fell into sin. Sin and sickness came upon the human race because of Adam's disobedience.

"Wherefore, as by one man sin entered into the world, and death by sin; and so death passed upon all men, for that all have sinned." Romans 5:12

B. Sickness and disease are part of the curse of disobedience (Deuteronomy 28:1-61).

C. Christ, who redeemed us from the curse of the law, bore our sins and our sicknesses on the cross (Galatians 3:13).

"Himself took our infirmities, and bare our sicknesses" Matthew 8:17

II. ARE THERE DIFFERENT CAUSES FOR SICKNESS AND DISEASE?

Yes!! ". . . the curse causeless shall not come." Proverbs 26:2

A. There are causes in the _____ realm such as carelessness in observing natural laws, eating poorly, getting an improper amount of rest and exercise and contracting a virus (I Corinthians 3:16-17; Philippians 2:25-30).

B. There are causes in the _____ realm, such as worry, anxiety, fear, stress and lack of forgiveness (bitterness).

C. There are causes in the _____ realm where sickness can be associated with judgment for sin (I Cor. 12:29-30) or a period of spiritual testing (Job 2:5-8).

III. WHY IS IT IMPORTANT TO DISCERN THE CAUSE FOR OUR SICKNESSES?

It is important to discern the cause because permanent healing can only be obtained if the true cause is dealt with and removed.

A. A person may need to begin to take better care of his physical body.

B. The thing that is causing the stress, fear or anxiety must be dealt with.

C. The sin that is leading to judgment must be repented of and forsaken.

D. True patience and faith must be cultivated during special dealings of God.

IV. HOW DO WE KNOW THAT IT IS GOD'S WILL TO HEAL?

We know it is God's will to heal because:

A. God refers to Himself as our doctor (Exodus 15:26).

B. God's restoration and sanctification involves the whole man (I Thessalonians 5:23).

C. Jesus healed all who came to Him (Luke 4:40).

D. Healing is part of the message of the Kingdom (Luke 9:1-2).

E. Jesus came to destroy the works of the devil (I John 3:8).

F. Healing is one of the signs that follow true believers (Mark 16:17-18).

"Beloved, I wish above all things that thou mayest prosper and be in health, even as thy soul prospereth." (III John 2)

V. WHAT ARE SOME SPIRITUAL HINDRANCES TO RECEIVING HEALING?

There are many reasons why healing may not come to us. At times it is totally beyond man's ability to know (Deuteronomy 29:29). Nevertheless, it is always good to examine our hearts to see if there is any trace of things that the Bible indicates may hinder divine healing.

A. An unforgiving spirit (Matthew 18:23-35).

B. Unconfessed sin (James 5:14-16).

C. Persistent unbelief (Mark 6:5-6; Matthew 9:29).

D. Not discerning the Lord's Body (I Corinthians 11:29-33).

E. Purposeful disobedience and rebellion (Exodus 15:26; Proverbs 4:20-22).

F. A sharp tongue (Proverbs 12:18).

G. Improper marital relationships (I Peter 3:1-7).

H. Satanic resistance (Daniel 10:12-13).

VI. *WHAT ARE SOME MEANS BY WHICH HEALING CAN BE RECEIVED?*

A. There are natural means, including diet, exercise and disciplined life (Proverbs 17:22; I Timothy 4:8).

B. There is the medical profession, which is certainly used of God (Matthew 9:12).

C. In addition, there are spiritual avenues of healing that God put in the church. These include the following:

1. Simple _____ to God by the sick person (James 5:13; Hebrews 11:6).

2. Laying on of believers' _____ (Mark 16:18).

.3. Anointing with _____ by elders of the church (James 5:14).

4. Through the _____ (Matthew 8:5-13; Psalms 107:20).

5. Through the _____ the Lord (I Corinthians 11:23-32).

6. Being ministered to by someone operating the _____ healing (I Corinthians 12:9).

7. Being ministered to by someone with the _____ healing (I Corinthians 12:28).

8. Through special and miraculous means (Mark 7:31-37; 8:22-26; John 9:1-7; Acts 19:11-12; 5:15-16).

Conclusion: Divine healing is one of Christ's ornaments for the Church, which is His bride. It is the children's bread (Matthew 15:21-28). Many times we fail to experience what is rightfully ours because we do not give God the chance to prove Himself in these areas. As Christians, we ought to determine to go to the Lord, our Maker, first when we need healing and strength. As we do, we will experience the Lord in a new way: ". . . the Lord that healeth thee."

13

Gifts of the Spirit

Purpose: The purpose of this lesson is to bring understanding, to remove any fear or misunderstanding and to give the believer guidelines for the expression of the gifts of the Spirit in the local church.

Key Verse: "Now there are diversities of gifts, but the same spirit . . . but the manifestation of the Spirit is given to every man to profit withal. For to one is given by the Spirit the word of wisdom; to another the word of knowledge by the same Spirit; to another faith by the same Spirit; to another the gifts of healing by the same Spirit; to another the working of miracles; to another prophecy; to another discerning of spirits; to another divers kinds of tongues; to another the interpretation of tongues: but all these worketh that one and the selfsame Spirit, dividing to every man severally as he will." I Corinthians 12:4, 7-11 KJV

I. WHAT IS MEANT BY "GIFTS OF THE SPIRIT"?

There are many gifts that are part of the experience of the believer. All of God's gifts are free, unearned and unmerited by man, but graciously given by God. The "gifts of the Spirit" outlined in I Corinthians 12 are to be distinguished from other gifts of God in the following ways:

A. These gifts are distinctly attributed to the Holy Spirit as the source (I Corinthians 12:4, 7-11).

B. These gifts are a manifestation or "shining forth" of the Spirit who dwells within the believer (I Corinthians 12:7).

C. These gifts are supernatural in character, not simply an extension or refinement of natural abilities or powers.

D. These gifts are distributed at the direction of the Holy Spirit to meet specific needs at specific times (I Corinthians 12:11).

E. The "gifts of the Spirit", therefore, are supernatural endowments given to the believer at the direction of the Holy Spirit to meet particular needs at particular times.

II. *WHAT ARE THE GIFTS OF THE SPIRIT?*

A. Gifts of Revelation — God communicating His mind to the Church.

  1. Widsom — The gift of the Word of Wisdom is the God-given ability to perceive supernatural wisdom from God when it is needed (Matthew 22:15-22).

  2. Knowledge — The gift of the Word of Knowledge is the God-given ability to receive from God, by revelation, facts and information which are humanly impossible to know (John 4:17-19).

  3. Discerning of Spirits — The gift of Discerning of Spirits is the God-given ability to recognize what spirit is behind different manifestations or activities. The gift also includes the God-given ability to challenge or cope with spirits (Acts 16:16-18).

B. Gifts of Inspiration — God speaking to the Church.

  1. Tongues — The gift of Tongues is a God-given ability which enables a believer to speak in a language which he does not know (Acts 2:1-17).

  2. Interpretation — The gift of Interpretation of Tongues is the God-given ability to bring forth, in a known tongue, a message which is given in an unknown tongue (Daniel 5:25-28).

  3. Prophecy — To prophesy is the ability to speak forth a message from God which is received from the Holy Spirit as it is brought forth (Acts 11:28; 21:10-11).

C. Gifts of Demonstration — God doing or acting in the Church.

  1. Faith — The gift of Faith is a God-given ability to believe God for the impossible (Acts 3:11, 13-16).

  2. Healing — The Gift of Healing is the God-given ability to impart healing for the physical body at certain, specific times (Acts 28:8-10).

  3. Miracles — The gift of Miracles is a God-given ability to perform the impossible (Acts 20:9-12; 13:8-12).

III. *HOW DO THESE GIFTS OPERATE?*

When it comes to the gifts of the Spirit, we see the Spirit of God and man working together as co-laborers.

A. There is the Spirit's part relative to the gifts.

  1. The Spirit takes the initiative as the giver (I Corinthians 12:11, 18, 28).

  2. The Spirit will always do His part.

B. There is man's part relative to the gifts.

  1. We should be totally _____ to the Lord (Romans 6:1-2, 13).

  2. We should _____ to be used in this realm (I Corinthians 14:1; 12:31).

  3. We should _____ all we can about the gifts (I Corinthians 12:1; Hosea 4:6).

  4. We should _____ to be used in the gifts (I Corinthians 14:13; Matthew 7:11).

5. We should maintain _____ and dispel unbelief (Romans 12:6; Mark 6:5-6).

6. We should not neglect, but _____ the gifts (I Timothy 4:14; II Timothy 1:6).

IV. WHAT GUIDELINES SHOULD GOVERN THE OPERATION OF THE GIFTS?

God gives many principles that anyone wanting to operate in the gifts should follow, realizing the vessel is responsible for the manner in which the gift is exercised.

A. The gift must be used for the purpose of edifying or _____ the Body of Christ (I Corinthians 14:3-5, 12, 17-26).

1. Will this strengthen the Body of Christ?

2. Will this bring comfort?

B. The gift must be operated decently and in order (I Corinthians 14:27, 29, 33, 40).

1. Is this _____ flowing with what God is saying?

2. Is this the best _____ to function in this gift?

3. Does my _____ of presentation add or detract from the message?

C. The gifts of the Spirit are to be balanced by the fruit of the Spirit. The gifts of the Spirit bring to us the ability of God. The fruit of the Spirit brings the character of God. We must have both the ability and the character of God in balance to bring life.

1. Love — Are you interested in the well-being of others (I Corinthians 13)?

2. Joy — Do you find your joy in building up others (II Corinthians 7:4)?

3. Peace — Are you at peace with the family of God (Matthew 5:22-24)?

4. Longsuffering — Are you willing to wait for the right time (II Timothy 4:2)?

5. Gentleness — Does it flow or interrupt? Is it pushy or gentle (James 3:17)?

6. Meekness — Are you ministering in true humility (I Peter 5:5)?

7. Goodness — Is your personal life in accord with God's Word (Isaiah 52:11)?

8. Self-control — Are you willing to limit yourself to the prescribed guidelines (I Corinthians 14:32)?

9. Faith — Has God told you to say or do this (Galatians 3:2, 5)?

D. A summary guideline to follow is: when operating the gifts of the Spirit, obey the moving of the Spirit which operates according to the Word of God on the basis of love and edification.

V. *WHAT ARE SOME MISCONCEPTIONS ABOUT THE GIFTS OF THE SPIRIT?*

A. Some feel that the gifts of the Spirit are an indication of God's approval on a life or a church assembly. However, the gifts of God are not earned or deserved; God gives gifts to meet the needs of His people and they can be misused and abused by man (Matthew 7:21-23).

B. Some feel that the gifts of the Spirit are an indication of spiritual maturity. However, the gifts are not to be seen as something that is only available to the "superspiritual", but these signs should follow those who believe (Mark 16:17-20).

Conclusion: The gifts of the Spirit are part of the equipment given to the Church by the Spirit so that the Church might be a supernatural influence in the world today. Believers should not be afraid of these realms but should look to the Lord each day for the supernatural enablements of the Spirit to face the individual and unique challenges that are a part of our everyday life and experience.

14

Worship and Praise

Purpose: The purpose of this lesson is to give the believer understanding concerning his God-given responsibility as a priest unto God to offer up spiritual sacrifices to God in praise, worship and thanksgiving and to inspire the believer toward a more intelligent expression of that worship.

Key Verse: "By Him therefore let us offer the sacrifice of praise to God continually, that is, the fruit of our lips giving thanks to His name. But to do good and to communicate forget not: for with such sacrifices God is well pleased." Hebrews 13:15-16 KJV

I. WHAT IS WORSHIP?

The word "worship" means, literally, "to bow yourself down" or "to extend yourself toward." It carries with it the idea of adoration, admiration and intense love. Every individual in the world worships someone or something and their entire lifestyle is an expression and an outworking of that worship. Every individual is bowing down to and extending themselves toward someone or something. If it is not God that they are worshipping, the focus of their whole life will be improper.

II. WHAT FORM OF WORSHIP IS PRESCRIBED FOR THE NEW TESTAMENT CHURCH?

Some people will say that it does not matter how you worship as long as you are sincere. The Bible seems to indicate, however, that God is very much concerned about both the sincerity of our hearts and the actual form in which that worship is expressed.

A. New Testament worship is to be worship in _____ (John 4:21-24).

B. New Testament worship is to be worship in _____ (John 4:21-24; Isaiah 29:13).

C. New Testament worship is according to the pattern of David's tabernacle (Acts 15:15-17). There are several reasons why this is the case:

   1. Paul quotes from the Psalms describing the worship expression of those who will be saved (Romans 15:9-11).

   2. The Psalms of David were a vital part of the New Testament worship expression (Colossians 3:16; Ephesians 5:19).

   3. James professed that the Church was the expression of the rebuilt tabernacle of David (Acts 15:15-17).

   4. Many New Testament passages imply a similar expression in worship (Acts 2:47; 3:8; 16:25; 24:14; I Thessalonians 5:16-21; I Timothy 2:8; Hebrews 13:15-16; I Peter 2:9).

   5. This is also the form of worship in heaven (Revelation 4:9-11; 5:9-11; 7:11-12; 11:16-17; 15:3-4; 19:1-6).

III. WHAT CHARACTERIZED THE WORSHIP IN DAVID'S TABERNACLE?

A. It was _____ (II Chronicles 29:25-29). In other words, they did not say the same formula over and over again; nor was there necessarily a prescribed order of worship that became a set form.

B. It was from the _____ (Psalms 86:12; 111:1). This is the only kind of worship God has ever desired.

C. It was expressed out of personal _____ and _____

   _____ (Psalms 51:15-17).

D. It was regular and _____ (Psalms 34:1; 72:15; 119:164; 145:2).

E. It was _____ with some opportunity for individual expression (I Chronicles 6:31-32; 15:16-18).

F. It had a strong emphasis on _____ (Psalms 148-150).

IV. WHAT FORMS DID WORSHIP TAKE IN DAVID'S TABERNACLE?

Since God has made man to be a three-part being (spirit, soul and body), He has given to man various ways to get himself totally involved in expressing worship to God (Luke 10:27). David outlines at least nine ways to worship in the Psalms.

A. We worship God with our _____ .

   1. With audible praise (Psalms 34:1; 40:16; 42:4; 66:8).

   2. With singing (Psalms 47:6; 61:8; 68:4; 104:33).

   3. With shouting (Psalms 5:11; 32:11; 35:27).

B. We worship God with our _____ .

   1. By lifting hands (Psalms 63:4; 119:48; 134:2; 141:2).

   2. By clapping hands (Psalms 47:1; 98:8).

   3. By playing musical instruments (Psalms 33:2-3; 57:8; 150:3-6).

C. We worship God with our very _____ .

   1. By standing (Psalms 135:2; 134:1)

   2. By dancing (Psalms 30:11; 149:3; 150:4).

   3. By bowing or kneeling (Psalms 95:6).

V. WHY DO WE MAKE SUCH AN EMPHASIS ON WORSHIP?

A. Because worship is commanded by God (Psalms 22:23).

B. Because God is worthy of our worship and praise (Psalms 18:3).

C. Because worship glorifies God (Psalms 50:23).

D. Because it helps us to develop our love relationship with God (Mark 12:30).

E. Because it releases the power of God's presence (Psalms 22:3).

F. Because we become like what we worship (Psalms 106:19-20; II Corinthians 3:18).

G. Because it is the proper way to come before God (Psalms 100:1-4).

H. Because it helps us to become God-centered instead of self-centered (Isaiah 26:3).

I. Because it is part of our priestly ministry unto the Lord (I Peter 2:5-9).

J. Because it is a definite sign of life (Psalms 115:17; Isaiah 38:19).

VI. WHAT HAPPENS WHEN WE WORSHIP?

Whenever we respond in obedience to the Lord, by our faith we put certain spiritual laws into operation for us. Therefore, we can expect certain results in spiritual realms.

A. Victory over our enemies (II Chronicles 20:1-30).

B. Release from bondages (Acts 16:16-34; Jonah 1:17-2:10).

C. Inner peace and joy (I Samuel 16:14-23).

D. The breaking up of large problems (Joshua 6:1-20).

E. Special protection from enemies (Isaiah 4:5-6).

F. A special manifestation of God's presence (II Chronicles 5:12-14).

VII. WHAT MAIN GUIDELINES SHOULD GOVERN OUR WORSHIP?

While there should be a certain spontaneity to our worship there are still certain guidelines that make worship most beneficial to all.

A. Total involvement (Psalms 134:1; 113:1). Worship is not meant for only a few, but all of God's people.

B. Unity of expression (Psalms 133). While there is a proper place for individual expression, public worship is a corporate expression and all should follow the designated worship leader.

C. Orderliness (I Corinthians 14:40). The guidelines established by the leadership should be carefully observed.

D. Edification (I Corinthians 14:26). All things done in the corporate gathering should be done to build up the people of God.

Conclusion: God's people were created to be a people of worship and praise. Worship and praise help us to keep all of life in proper perspective and to serve to remind us that we are first and foremost the servants of the King of Kings and Lord of Lords (Rev. 4:10-11).

15

Evangelism

Purpose: The purpose of this lesson is to convince every believer of their personal responsibility to be a witness of the Lord Jesus Christ and to equip them with a basic knowledge of the Gospel message that they might be able to share it with others.

Key Verse: "Go ye therefore, and teach all nations, baptizing them in the name of the Father, and of the Son, and of the Holy Ghost: teaching them to observe all things whatsoever I have commanded you: and, lo, I am with you always, even unto the end of the world. Amen." Matthew 28:19-20 KJV

I. WHAT DOES THE WORD "EVANGELISM" MEAN?

The Greek word from which we get our English word "evangelism" simply means "to tell" or "to announce _____ ." In Christian circles this word refers to the "good news" or the Gospel of Jesus Christ.

II. WHY IS THE "GOOD NEWS" NECESSARY?

A. God, who is absolutely righteous and holy, created man in His own likeness and image (Genesis 1:26-28).

B. The first man, Adam, fell into sin and out of fellowship with God, thus marring the image in which he was created (Genesis 3:1-21).

C. Because we are all offspring of Adam and we were made in the image of our father Adam (Genesis 5:3), every man born into the world is born _____ and "shapen in iniquity" (Psalms 51:5; Romans 3:9-12; 5:12).

1. All are children of _____ (Ephesians 2:3).

2. All are _____ (Romans 3:19).

3. All have a rendezvous with _____ (Hebrews 9:27; Romans 5:12).

4. All are _____ in trespasses and sins (Ephesians 2:1).

5. All are _____ from the life of God (Ephesians 4:18).

6. All are _____ to the law of God (Romans 8:7).

D. Man has been separated from God for so long that he has become used to the unnatural and he actually

loves _____ rather than light (John 3:19).

E. There is no possible way for a sinful, disobedient man to dwell or have intimate fellowship with a holy and absolutely righteous God.

III. WHAT IS THE "GOOD NEWS"?

A. God took the initiative in bringing man back into fellowship with Himself by sending Jesus Christ to be the head of a new race (Galatians 3:26-29).

   1. Christ was also the image of God (Hebrews 1:3).
   2. Christ did not fall into sin as Adam did (Hebrews 4:15).
   3. Christ received the full penalty for sin in Himself, though undeserving (Romans 5:8).

B. All who receive Christ as Saviour accept the finished work of Calvary as the only way to salvation, repent of their sins and acknowledge the lordship of Jesus Christ, receive the new birth experience and are born into Christ (John 3:1-5; Acts 2:38-39; John 14:6).

   1. In Christ we are made _____ (Romans 4:5, 22-25).

   2. In Christ there is _____ condemnation (Romans 8:1-2).

   3. In Christ we are conformed to the _____ (Romans 8:28-30).

   4. In Christ we have _____ with God (Romans 5:1).

   5. In Christ we have _____ to the Father (Romans 5:2).

C. Man is ultimately restored to a place of full fellowship with the Father and becomes a partaker of the riches of His glory (Ephesians 1:18; Colossians 1:27; Romans 9:23).

D. God has provided one way of salvation for all men, whether Jew or Gentile (Romans 3:10; 5:21).

IV. WHO IS RESPONSIBLE TO TELL THE "GOOD NEWS"?

A. God's way of salvation is not discovered by man; it comes to him by revelation and must be

_____ to him from the revealed Word of God (Romans 10:17-18; 16:25-26).

B. The Gospel message has been entrusted to the _____ (Matthew 28:18-20; Ephesians 3:9-11).

C. _____ are responsible to respond to the command of Jesus, for the Church is comprised of people (Mark 16:5-20; Acts 1:8).

V. WHAT DOES THE NEW TESTAMENT TEACH US ABOUT OUR RESPONSIBILITY TO TELL THE "GOOD NEWS"?

A. The primary ministry of Jesus was to evangelize (Luke 4:18; 43; Matthew 11:5; Luke 8:1).

B. The ministry of those whom Jesus sent out was evangelism (Luke 9:6).

C. Paul was ready to preach the gospel everywhere (Romans 1:15).

D. The early church recognized its responsibility in evangelism (Acts 5:42; 8:4, 12, 25, 36, 40; 13:1-5; 14:7, 21; 16:10, etc.).

E. The good news must be shared, for this is the only way it is spread (Romans 10:12-18).

F. There is a necessity that we all be involved in this area (I Corinthians 9:16).

G. We should not preach only when we get paid for it (I Corinthians 9:18).

H. Paul gives special commendation to the churches at Rome and Thessalonica for their efforts in evangelizing in their communities and beyond their borders (Romans 1:8; I Thessalonians 1:8).

Conclusion: The Kingdom of God is a kingdom of light, as opposed to the darkness of Satan's kingdom. God is Light (I John 1:5) and so is His Kingdom. The very nature of light is that it is outgoing. Light is diffusive, penetrating, searching. Light spreads itself all over space and fills all things. God's Kingdom is also like this. It is the very nature of God and His Kingdom to spread itself and expose all areas of darkness.

Since this is the case, it is not at all strange that the Church of Jesus Christ, which is God's vehicle and time-manifestation of the Kingdom of God, would be involved in evangelism. The only "good news" in this world of darkness is the Light of the Gospel of Jesus Christ. As members of the Body of Christ we are responsible to get the Word out.

The Believer and Government

Purpose: The purpose of this lesson is to help the believer see his responsibility in differing spheres of authority and to be able to live a balanced lifestyle, keeping allegiance to each in proper perspective.

Key Verse: "Let every soul be subject unto the higher powers. For there is no power but of God: the powers that be are ordained of God. Whosoever therefore resisteth the power, resisteth the ordinance of God: and they that resist shall receive to themselves damnation." Romans 13:1-2 KJV

I. WHAT AREAS OF GOVERNMENT HAVE BEEN ESTABLISHED BY GOD TO HELP MAINTAIN ORDER AND BRING HIS ETERNAL PURPOSE TO FULFILLMENT?

In the beginning, God created the heavens and the earth and, having done so, declared His purpose to have a man in His image who would be fruitful and multiply and subdue the earth for divine purposes.

To help accomplish this purpose, God established three human institutions. All authority starts, first, with God. It is then distributed to whomever God wills.

A. The family (Genesis 2:18-24). God established the family as a context in which man would realize the eternal purpose for which he was created. The family is the God-ordained context for the establishment and development of:

1. God-centered relationship and fellowship.

2. God-like character in man.

3. God-ordained ministry and function.

4. Natural and spiritual reproduction.

B. The civil government (Genesis 9:1-6; John 19:11). God established governmint for the purpose of giving order to society. Civil government would do this through the following means:

    1. Punishing the wicked (Romans 13:3-4).

    2. Supporting and honoring good behavior (Ecclesiastes 8:11; Psalm 72:4, 12-14).

C. The church (Matthew 16:18-19). God established the church, or the assembly of the saints, to be his spokesman in the earth, the equipper of the house and the conscience to the nation to see God's purpose fulfilled.

II. WHAT IS GOD'S RELATIONSHIP TO THESE ESTABLISHED INSTITUTIONS?

While each of these institutions is given tremendous liberty by God to function within their spheres, it is clear that:

A. God holds supreme authority over all (Daniel 4:34-35; Matthew 28:18).

B. God will call all to give an account (Matthew 25:14-30).

C. Governments are all servants of God to do His will (Romans 13:4).

III. WHAT AREAS OF INVOLVEMENT DO NOT BELONG TO CIVIL GOVERNMENT?

God has given to each institution certain responsibilities to fulfill. To the civil authorities He has given the judicial responsibility of upholding right and punishing evil, as God defines it. In addition, it can be seen that God supported the right of the civil authorities to raise an army for military defense (I Samuel 8:11-12, 20, 22). But there are many areas in which God has *not* given authority to the state:

A. The state is not to be involved in corruptions, using their office for gain and exploiting the people (Deuteronomy 16:19; 17:16-17; I Kings 12).

B. The state is not responsible for the raising and educating of children. This is clearly a parental responsibility (Genesis 18:19; Proverbs 22:6; Ephesians 6:4).

C. The state is not responsible for welfare and the care of the aged, widows and orphans. This responsibility is clearly given to the individual, the family and, ultimately, the church (I Corinthians 16:1-2; Job 29:11-16; 31:5-22; I Timothy 5:4-10).

Sometimes, a government will overstep its jurisdiction. At that point, each person must determine how they believe they must respond to such action or whether any response is required at all. The Christian must always maintain a biblical balance in these areas. The Bible teaches us to be submissive to the ruling authorities over us; yet, at the same time, we must hold our obedience to God above that (Romans 13:1-4; Acts 5:28-29).

IV. IN WHAT WAYS SHOULD THE CHRISTIAN BE INVOLVED IN THE AFFAIRS OF CIVIL GOVERNMENT?

Every believer has the responsibility of properly relating to all forms of government in the home, the church and society. In the civil government realm a good Christian citizen involves himself in the following:

A. _____ for all in authority (I Timothy 2:1-2).

B. Giving due _____ to authorities at all times (Romans 13:7).

C. _____ to the decisions of the state so long as they do not require us to sin and, thus, violate God's higher law (I Peter 2:13-14).

D. _____ in all state and local elections (Matthew 5:13-14; Ezekiel 3:16-21).

E. _____ as required by law (Matthew 22:17-21; Romans 13:7).

F. Lifting a public voice _____ (Matthew 5:13-14; Ezekiel 3:16-21).

G. Being informed and understanding _____ (Ephesians 5:15-16; II Corinthians 2:11).

H. Being informed about the _____ of one's nation (Acts 16:37; 22:25).

I. Running for political office in a system that allows it.

Conclusion: God is the only one who has the authority to rule over men (Psalm 25:7). However, God delegates His authority to whomever He wills in order to see His purposes established in the earth (Daniel 5:21). God expects all men to cooperate with those to whom He has given authority insofar as those authorities do not use their authority to force those under their charge to violate the direct Word of God. All Christians should be model citizens when it comes to obeying the law, paying their taxes and being involved in the political process. All Christians should pray daily that the purposes of God would be established through the governments that are placed over them.

Study Questions

Lessons 9-16

LESSON 9 — PRAYER AND FASTING

1. All believers should have a specific time set aside for _____ prayer.

2. The three realms in which every believer should practice prayer include (1) _____

_____ , (2) _____ and (3) _____ .

LESSON 10 — CHRISTIAN STEWARDSHIP

3. Stewardship is the practice of _____

_____

_____

_____ .

4. The five realms in which stewardship is to be recognized and practiced include _____

(1) _____ ,

(2) _____ , (3) _____ ,

(4) _____ , (5) _____ .

LESSON 11 — STEWARDSHIP OF FINANCES

5. Tithing refers to the practice of giving _____

_____ back to the Lord for His work.

6. Some New Testament principles of giving indicate that we are to give (1) _____

_____ (2) _____

(3) _____ (4) _____ (5) _____

(6) _____ (7) _____ (8) _____

(9) _____ (10) _____ .

LESSON 12 — DIVINE HEALING

7. The three causes for sickness and disease are (1) _____

(2) _____ and (3) _____ .

8. Some hindrances to healing include (1) _____ ,

(2) _____ , (3) _____ ,

(4) _____ , (5) _____ ,

(6) _____ , (7) _____ .

LESSON 13 — GIFTS OF THE SPIRIT

9. In order that the gifts operate decently and in order, the person operating the gifts must consider the

(1) _____ , (2) _____

and (3) _____ .

10. The basic guideline for operating the gifts is to obey the moving of the Spirit which operates _____

_____ on the basis of _____ .

LESSON 14 — WORSHIP AND PRAISE

11. Six things that characterized the worship in David's tabernacle are that worship was

(1) _____ , (2) _____ ,

(3) _____ , (4) _____ ,

(5) _____ , (6) _____ .

12. Four main guidelines should govern our worship, including (1) _____

_____ , (2) _____ ,

(3) _____ , (4) _____ .

LESSON 15 — EVANGELISM

13. The Greek word from which we get our English word "evangelism" simply means _____

_____ .

14. God's way of salvation is not discovered by man; it comes to him by _____

_____ and must be _____ .

LESSON 16 — THE BELIEVER AND GOVERNMENT

15. The three spheres of government that have been established by God include (1) _____

_____ , (2) _____ , and (3) _____ .

16. The two main functions of civil government are punishing _____

and supporting and honoring _____ .

17

RESTORING THE CHURCH — PRINCIPLES OF CHURCH LIFE

The Home

Purpose: The purpose of this lesson is to help the believer appreciate the tremendous value that God places on the home, to see how vitally connected the restoration of the home is to the restoration of the Church and to understand God's basic order and design for the home.

Key Verse: " Except the Lord build the house, they labour in vain that build it: except the Lord keep the city, the watchman waketh but in vain. It is vain for you to rise up early, to sit up late, to eat the bread of sorrows: for so He giveth his beloved sleep. Lo, children are an heritage of the Lord: and the fruit of the womb is his reward. As arrows are in the hands of a mighty man; so are children of the youth. Happy is the man that hath his quiver full of them: they shall not be ashamed, but they shall speak with the enemies in the gate." Psalm 127 KJV

I. HOW IS A HOUSE ESTABLISHED?

Just as a material house does not come together by accident, but by design, so it is with our families.

A. A house must be built by godly wisdom (Psalm 127:1; Proverbs 14:1).

B. A house must have a proper foundation (Matthew 7:24-27).

C. A house must have divinely instituted government, which is its structure (Ephesians 6:1-4; I Peter 3:1-7; Psalm 68:5).

II. WHAT IS THE ORDER OF HEADSHIP IN THE HOME?

There is an order of headship in the home even as there is in the Church and the godhead. This is God's chain of command (I Corinthians 11:3; Colossians 1:18; Ephesians 5:23-25). In the home God's established order is: husband, wife and children.

III. *DOES HEADSHIP IMPLY SUPERIORITY?*

Absolutely not! All persons of the godhead are equal in person and nature and yet the Son recognizes the headship of the Father in terms of role and function (I Corinthians 11:3; 15:28). The Bible clearly teaches that, in Christ, there is neither male nor female, and that both are equal in person and nature before the Lord (Galatians 3:28). But it is equally true that God has prescribed distinct roles and functions for each (I Corinthians 11:3).

A. Headship does not mean:

    1. Dictatorship
    2. Inequality of person and value
    3. Inferiority of womankind
    4. Superiority of mankind

B. Headship does mean:

    1. Ultimate responsibility. The man is ultimately responsible to lead, guide and provide for his home in all areas (I Timothy 5:8).

    2. Ultimate accountability. God will hold the man accountable for the state of the family at the judgment seat of Christ (Hebrews 13:17).

IV. *WHAT ARE TO BE THE PRIMARY FUNCTIONS OF THE FAMILY MEMBERS?*

A. The primary role and function of the husband and father.

    1. The man is to be submitted to Christ as his head (I Corinthians 11:3).

    2. The man is to provide for the home naturally and spiritually (I Timothy 5:8; Exodus 12:3).

    3. The man is to be the source of love in the home (Ephesians 5:25; Colossians 3:19).

    4. The man is to unselfishly give himself to his wife and family as Christ did for the church (Ephesians 5:25-31).

    5. The man is to use his authority to serve each family member (John 13:3-4; Philippians 2:5-8).

    6. The man is to treat his wife with dignity and honor as he would his own flesh (I Peter 3:7; Ephesians 5:29).

    7. The man is to receive his wife as God's gift and an helper suitable for him (Genesis 2:18-24).

The man characterized in Ephesians 5 is a man of love and gentleness who is willing to give himself unreservedly to the welfare and strengthening of other family members. He is a giving person who nourishes and cherishes all under his care providing for them all things that make for healthy growth and happiness.

B. The primary role and function of the wife and mother.

    1. The woman must be willing to voluntarily receive her husband's ordained authority (I Corinthians 11:3; Ephesians 5:22-24).

    2. The woman is to honor her husband (I Peter 3:6).

    3. The woman is to maintain a meek and quiet spirit (I Peter 3;1-5).

4. The woman is to be a complement to her husband (Genesis 2:18).

5. The woman is to be given to hospitality (Hebrews 13;1, 2).

6. The woman is to be a creative homemaker (Proverbs 31).

The woman characterized in Proverbs 31 is a commendable wife and mother who is industrious, self-disciplined, orderly, charitable, given to hospitality, who lives for her home and family. She is a woman of virtue because she is spiritually minded and she takes her home seriously.

C. The primary role of the children in the home.

1. Children are the special gifts of God to a man and woman.

   a. Children are the _____ of the Lord (Psalm 127:3-5).

   b. Children are as _____ of the mighty.

   c. Children are as ___ _____ plants (Psalm 128:3).

   d. Children are the Lord's _____ (Psalm 127:3).

   e. Children are a _____ (Proverbs 17:6).

2. Children are servants in the home and are to obey their parents (Ephesians 6:1).

3. Children are to give honor and respect to their parents (Ephesians 6:2).

4. Children are to receive correction when necessary (Proverbs 13:24; 22:6; 29:15; 22:15; 23:14; 20:11; 23:13; 20:30).

V. WHAT ARE SOME KEYS TO SUCCESSFUL FAMILY LIVING?

There are no magic formulas to success in the home. However, if certain attitudes and qualities prevail among all family members God will bless the house in a special way.

A. Love. When each member of the family is motivated by selflessness the family problems will be minimized drastically (I Corinthians 13:4-7).

B. Servant Heart. When each member of the family treats the other members as more important than themselves and serves gladly, everyone's needs will be met (Philippians 2:3).

C. Mutual Submission. As family members learn to yield their rights to others, peace will prevail (Ephesians 5:21).

D. Communication. Every member of the family must be committed to open, honest, edifying communication (Ephesians 4:29).

E. Forgiveness. Every home has abundant opportunity to exercise this virtue. Individuals who fail to forgive and apologize freely will live in torment (Matthey 18:23-25).

Conclusion: It is clear that God wants all of our homes to be an example to the world of kingdom principles in operation. It is one place where we can build according to God's pattern and expect to see the fruit that God has promised. Every Christian should realize this and do all they can to make their home a place of righteousness, peace and joy in the Holy Ghost (Romans 14:17).

18

The Church

Purpose: The purpose of this lesson is to help the believer understand the importance of the Church as it relates to God's overall purpose, to see how God wants to use the Church as His vehicle to accomplish this purpose and to appreciate the great restoration that God is effecting in the Church these days to make His purpose a reality.

Key Verse: "And I say also unto thee, that thou art Peter, and upon this rock I will build my church; and the gates of hell shall not prevail against it. And I will give unto thee the keys of the kingdom of heaven: and whatsoever thou shalt bind on earth shall be bound in heaven: and whatsoever thou shalt loose on earth shall be loosed in heaven." Matthew 16:18-19 KJV

I. WHAT IS THE CHURCH?

    A. The word "church" literally means, "the called out ones". The Church is not a _____

_____ but it consists of all those people who have been _____

" _____ " from the world, who have _____

themselves unto God and have _____ unto the Lord Jesus Christ for worship and fellowship (I Peter 2:4-10).

    B. The Church is God's present instrument, or vehicle, in the earth through which God desires to extend His kingdom and fulfill His purpose (Matthew 21:43; Ephesians 1:3-14; 3:9-11).

    C. The Church has two main aspects: the universal and the local.

        1. The universal Church consists of that company of believers in Christ in all ages, living and dead, who are distinct from the world by virtue of their calling in God (Ephesians 1:22; 3:21; 5:25-32).

2. The local Church consists of groups of believers in given localities which are marked out by:

    a. confession of faith,
    b. discipline of life,
    c. obedience in baptism,
    d. gathering to the person of Jesus Christ,
    e. having gifted ministries from Christ
    f. and keeping the memorial of the Lord.

They are always spoken of as complete units within themselves, which may voluntarily cooperate and fellowship with other local bodies (Acts 13:1; I Corinthians 1:2).

II. WHY IS IT IMPORTANT TO HAVE AN UNDERSTANDING OF THE UNIVERSAL, OR INVISIBLE, CHURCH?

It is important to understand the concept of the universal Church so that:

A. We can see our connection and mystical union with all believers of past ages who have run before us, realizing that they are counting on us to finish the race (Hebrews 12:1-2).

B. We can see that all believers in the world are really one in Christ. When one suffers we all suffer and when one rejoices we all rejoice (Acts 11:27-30; I Corinthians 12:26).

C. We can see that what God is doing is bigger than one local church, sect, denomination or people but includes every nation, kindred, tribe and tongue in each and every generation (II Peter 3:9; Revelation 5:9-10; 14:6-7).

III. WHY IS IT IMPORTANT TO HAVE AN UNDERSTANDING OF THE LOCAL CHURCH?

It is extremely important not to exalt the universal Church above the local Church in our practical living. The Bible uses the word "church" some 114 times and 96 references are clearly to the local Church. We must put the emphasis where God puts it for the following reasons:

A. It is in the local Church that we are going to put our _____ into practice. (Matthew 18:15-20).

B. It is in the local Church that we are going to find the dynamics to bring us to maturity (Ephesians 4:11-16).

C. It is in the local Church that our ministry and function is going to be realized (Romans 12:3-8; I Corinthians 12:18-28).

D. It is in the local Church we are going to find protection from deception (Psalm 91).

IV. WHAT ARE SOME OTHER NAMES AND TITLES GIVEN TO THE CHURCH?

A. The Israel of God (Galatians 6:16).

B. The Pillar and Ground of Truth (I Timothy 3:15).

C. The Temple of God (Ephesians 2:21-22).

D. The House of the Lord (Hebrews 3:1-4; I Timothy 3:15).

E. The Family of God (Ephesians 3:14-15).

F. The Household of Faith (Galatians 6:10).

G. The Body of Christ (Ephesians 1:20-23).

H. The Army of God (Ephesians 6:10-13; II Timothy 2:3-4).

I. The Bride of Christ (Ephesians 5:28-32; Revelation 19:6-9).

V. WHAT IS THE NATURE OF THE CHURCH THAT JESUS IS BUILDING TODAY?

The Church of Jesus Christ is going to take on the nature of its Builder and Maker. Nowhere in the Bible do we read of a defeated or failing Bride of Christ. Hence, we can expect the Church to be strong and glorious (Matthew 16:18-19).

A. The Church will be _____ unto the Lord (Ephesians 5:23-32).

B. The Church will be _____ (John 17:18-23).

C. The Church will be _____ (Matthew 16:18-19; Romans 16:20).

D. The Church will enter into _____ (Ephesians 1:20-24).

E. The Church will come to the measure of the stature of the _____

_____ (Ephesians 4:11-13).

VI. WHAT IS THE RELATIONSHIP OF THE CHURCH TO OTHER PARA-CHURCH ORGANIZATIONS?

The Bible is clear that it is through the vehicle, or instrument, of the Church that God is going to accomplish His great purpose. However, because the Church has not always been what it was supposed to be, many have become discouraged with the Church's ability to meet certain obvious needs. For this reason, caring and concerned individuals have, over the years, established missionary societies, orphanages, Christian businessmen's organizations and other like institutions to meet these pressing needs. As God continues to restore and strengthen His Church, the need for these organizations will diminish and the Church will be ministering to these needs.

Conclusion: Because of many negative experiences by Christians today, many have written off the Church as having nothing to offer them personally or the world in general. Unfortunately, the Church experiences that have offended them or otherwise caused them to become disillusioned were not in God's original design for His Church. When we get back to God's original plan and blueprint for the Church it will be the most exciting organization on the face of the earth. The challenge to God's people in these days is to get a vision of what the Church can be and put all of their faith and energy into seeing that vision become a reality.

19

Restoration of the Church

Purpose: The purpose of this lesson is to help the believer get a vision for what God wants to do in and through the church in these days so that they can intelligently commit themselves in time, energy and stewardship to the strengthening, rebuilding and development of a strong, united, victorious local church.

Key Verse: "Repent ye therefore, and be converted, that your sins may be blotted out, when the times of refreshing shall come from the presence of the Lord; and He shall send Jesus Christ, which before was preached unto you: whom the Heaven must receive until the times of restitution of all things, which God hath spoken by the mouth of all His holy prophets since the world began." Acts 3:19-21 KJV

I. WHAT DOES THE WORD "RESTORATION" MEAN?

A. The word restoration literally means to bring something back or to put something back into its former or original state. It means to repair, renew, to put back into existence or use. It means that whatever has been lost, misplaced or stolen is now put back into existence, a former condition or use.

B. When applied to the church the word restoration refers to the recovery to the church of truth that has been lost. It speaks of a reviving of New Testament Christianity and a renewing of New Testament experience.

II. WHAT IS THE NEED FOR "RESTORATION" IN THE EXPERIENCE OF THE CHURCH?

A. The general condition of the church today is much different than that of the early church.

1. The early church was a _____ church (Acts 2:40-41; 8:7, 39; 19:11-13).

2. The early church had a tremendous measure of _____ (Acts 2:42).

3. The early church had a high level of Christian _____ (Hebrews 6:1-2).

B. The church experienced a decline through the centuries.

1. Many lost their _____ (Revelation 2:1-7).

2. There was a decline in emphasis on the _____ .

3. There was a lessening of the dependance on the _____ .

4. There was a spirit of _____ that diluted the church.

C. Many doctrines were either lost to the church or declined to mere ritual and form.

1. The Gifts of the Spirit
2. The Fivefold Ministry
3. Plurality of Elders
4. Priesthood of All Believers
5. And many others

III. WHAT ARE GOD'S PROMISES CONCERNING RESTORATION?

A. God will restore His city to a place of faithfulness and righteousness (Isaiah 1:21-27).

B. God will accomplish this before the return of Christ (Acts 3:19-21).

1. The word "restitution" is synonymous with "restoration". This statement refers to the end of the Church Age when God will bring back to the Church those things which were lost. This time of restoration and restitution will immediately precede the second coming of Christ (Acts 3:21; Ecclesiastes 3:1; Acts 1:6-7; I Thessalonians 5:1).

2. The things to be restored before Christ's coming are those things specifically referred to in the Prophets. If the prophets made predictions concerning this time, then they will surely come to pass. The Church should be eagerly searching the prophetic Scriptures for clues to our position in God's timetable.

A *word of warning* is in order at this point. Some feel that the Devil will be restored. This is a typical example of the natural mind trying to interpret restoration apart from the prophets. Nowhere in the Scriptures can a prophetic voice be found predicting the restoration of Satan. Such thinking therefore must be rejected. This rule of interpretation should be applied to any restoration theory (See Revelation 20:10 and 14).

IV. WHAT ARE GOD'S PRINCIPLES THAT GOVERN RESTORATION?

A. God's restoration always involved returning _____ than was taken (Exodus 22:1-13; Luke 19:18).

B. God's restoration is always perfect and complete (Mark 3:5, 8:25).

V. WHAT DOES THE BIBLE TEACH CONCERNING THE RESTORATION OF THE NATURAL JEW?

A. God originally separated Israel to be the channel of His kingdom through which the Messiah would come (Galatians 3:19-29).

B. When Israel rejected the Messiah as a nation God took the administration of the kingdom from them and gave it to the church (Matthew 21:43).

C. When Israel rejected the Messiah they were cut off as branches from the tree of faith (Romans 11:17-24).

D. The Church of Jesus Christ is now the people of God and the Israel of God (Galatians 6:16).

E. Whenever natural Jews receive Christ as Saviour and Lord, they are grafted back into the tree of faith, they become part of the Israel of God and they become one with other Jews and Gentiles in the church, the body of Christ (Ephesians 2:11-22).

F. The Bible teaches a spiritual restoration of Israel by an outpouring of the Holy Spirit under the New Covenant. It is not a restoration of the Mosaic Covenant ritualism (Acts 2:17; Joel 2:28-32; Romans 10:1; 9-13; 11:23-26; Acts 16:31).

Conclusion: The Bible is basically a Bible of Restoration. Genesis, the "Book of Beginnings", shows us the origin of many things. The Revelation, the last book of the Bible, tells us the final state of all things. The Bible's basic plot is simple: it is the story of a God-created man who willfully violated God's love, thereby alienating himself from God. God then initiated a wonderful plan that would ultimately restore the fallen man to a relationship with his Creator. Between Genesis 3:24 and Revelation 21:3 and 4, we see the panorama of restoration in its fullest sense. It is in the church where we are going to see God finish this great and glorious plan. It is the church, the Bride of Christ, that will be prepared and ready for the Lord's return (Revelation 19:7).

Church Government

Purpose: The purpose of this lesson is to help the believer to understand the need for government, structure and order in the Church, to understand God's plan for that government and to rightly relate to that God-given authority in their lives.

Key Verse: "Obey them that have the rule over you, and submit yourselves: for they watch for your souls, as they that must give account, that they may do it with joy, and not with grief: for that is unprofitable for you." Hebrews 13:17 KJV

I. WHAT AREAS OF GOVERNMENT HAVE BEEN ESTABLISHED BY GOD?

The Bible identifies clearly three main areas of government in society: the home, civil government and Church authority (see I Corinthians 11:1-3; Romans 13; Hebrews 13:17). In this lesson we will deal with Church government.

II. WHAT ARE THREE MAIN BIBLE FACTS CONCERNING CHURCH GOVERNMENT?

A. The first fact that the Bible makes very clear is that God has established _____

_____ in His House, the Church.

1. With no government, no structure or order there is chaos, lawlessness, anarchy and disorder (Judges 17:6; 21:25; II Thessalonians 2:4; II Peter 2:10; I Corinthians 14:33, 40).

2. There are those that _____ in the House of God (Romans 12:8).

"Obey them that have the rule over you . . ." Hebrews 13:17

"Remember those which have the rule over you . . ." Hebrews 13:7

B. The second fact clearly revealed in the Scripture is that God identifies the rulers in His House as

_____ (I Timothy 5:17).

    1. God could have chosen any form of government for His House, dictatorship (one-man rule), democracy (rule by majority), central control (rule by headquarters) or many others.

    2. God clearly chose that His House be governed by _____

_____ .

        a. Plurality of elders means more than _____ (Acts 14:23; 20:17; James 5:14).

        b. Plurality of elders includes the idea of a _____ , or senior pastor (Acts 12:17; 21:18).

    3. Another name for elders used in the New Testament is the word " _____

_____ ". The word bishop simply means, "overseer" and describes the function that an elder has (Philippians 1:1; I Timothy 3:1).

C. The third main fact concerning Church government is that God determines the kind of individuals that are to be the rulers in His House (I Timothy 3:1-9; Titus 1:5-9).

    1. They must have proven _____ . . . blameless, temperate, sober, of good behavior, not given to wine, not greedy of money, not coveteous, not self-willed, a lover of good.

    2. They must have _____ . . . not a novice, just, holy, having a good report among the unsaved, able to teach, holding fast the faithful word, patient, able to convince with sound doctrine.

    3. They must have their _____ . . . husband of one wife, above reproach, children in submission, hospitable, ruling own house well.

    4. They must be _____ for an equipping ministry by the Holy Spirit . . . apostle, prophet, evangelist, pastor and teacher (Ephesians 4:11-13).

III. WHAT ARE THE RESPONSIBILITIES OF THE ELDERS TOWARD THE PEOPLE?

The responsibilities of the elders fall into three main categories:

A. _____ (I Thessalonians 5:12-14). This involves the general oversight of the ongoing affairs of the church. To rule means "to preside over, to superintend, to care for, to give attention to." The elders are to the church what parents are to the home. As rulers, therefore, they stand accountable before God for the state of the assembly (Heb. 13:17). God expects elders to rule with a spirit of gentleness (I Peter 5:2-3).

B. _____ (Acts 20:28-35). This involves feeding the flock, watching out for wolves, helping the weak, ministering to the sick and being an example for the sheep to follow.

C. _____ (I Timothy 3:2; Titus 1:9). By teaching sound doctrine, the elders are going to help bring stability to the Body and maturity to the saints so that all the members of the Body might become responsible with the use of their gifts, talents and ministries.

IV. *WHAT ARE THE MAIN RESPONSIBILITIES OF THE PEOPLE TOWARD THE ELDERS?*

God gives responsibilities both ways. If leaders are not righteous, the people groan; but if the people do not respond properly to their leaders, the leaders are grieved (Hebrews 13:17).

A. The people are to esteem elders highly (I Thessalonians 5:13).

B. The people are to submit themselves to Godly leadership (Hebrews 13:17).

C. The people are to financially support the elders (I Timothy 5:17-18; I Corinthians 9:11-14).

D. The people are to be careful about hastily charging an elder with wrongdoing (I Timothy 5:1, 19-20).

E. The people are to pray for their leaders (I Thessalonians 5:25).

Conclusion: It is not God's intention that the relationship between elders and the people be forced or strained. God wants His Church to be a family where all are able to enjoy the warmth of His presence in their midst. But God is a God of order and wants His family to reflect His nature. The structure is not intended to stifle the Body but to give it the strength and stability necessary to face the challenges of the coming days. God grant us all the grace that we need to flow together to the goodness of the Lord in the place where He has put us.

21

Laying On of Hands

Purpose: The purpose of this lesson is to familiarize the believers with a little-known doctrine that is foundational to the life of every believer and a source of impartation of great strength and blessing to the people of God when found in operation in the local church.

Key Verse: "Therefore leaving the principles of the doctrine of Christ, let us go on unto perfection; not laying again the foundation of repentance from dead works, and of faith toward God, of the doctrine of baptisms, and of laying on of hands, and of resurrection of the dead, and of eternal judgment. And this will we do, if God permit." Hebrews 6:1-3 KJV.

I. WHAT SPIRITUAL PRINCIPLE IS BEHIND THE DOCTRINE OF THE LAYING ON OF HANDS?

God often uses a physical, material element as a channel through which to accomplish a spiritual work. In baptism, God commands the use of a natural element (water) to effect a spiritual cleansing (Acts 22:16). In healing, God encourages the use of oil to confer spiritual strength (James 5:14). In both of these cases, the water or oil, in themselves, do nothing; but when they are used with the Word and with faith according to God's command they effect the desired results. When God chooses such a channel to use, He usually chooses a natural agent that is consistent with the spiritual work He wants to accomplish. Water is a natural cleansing agent; oil is a natural healing agent. God, however, uses these in connection with spiritual cleansing and healing.

II. WHAT IS THE SIGNIFICANCE OF THE HANDS IN THE BIBLE?

Certain natural things in the Bible clearly have a spiritual significance and application. God teaches spiritual truths with natural things (II Corinthians 4:18; Romans 1:20). In the Bible, hands are seen to be connected with spiritual power and strength.

A. The right hand of the Lord is seen as a source of _____ (Exodus 15:6; Psalms 20:6; Isaiah 62:8).

B. The hand of man is also seen as a source of _____ or strong aid (Psalms 76:5).

III. WHAT IS THE SIGNIFICANCE OF THE LAYING ON OF HANDS?

Throughout the Bible we see God using the hands of man in special ways and accomplishing various things. The anointed hands become the channel, the vehicle, the bridge by which something is transferred, or transmitted, from one person to another. Three key words that are often associated with this concept are:

A. Identification — Through the laying on of hands one party identifies, or associates, himself with the other.

    1. In the Old Testament, when the people laid their hands on the sacrificial animal that was to be killed, they were identifying themselves with that animal in its death (Leviticus 4:24).

    2. When the people of Israel laid hands on their leaders they were identifying with them as God's choice for them (Numbers 8:10).

B. Impartation — Through the laying on of hands one party imparts, or transfers, something to another.

    1. In the Old Testament, when the priest laid his hands on the scapegoat, the sins of the nation of Israel were imparted to the animal (Leviticus 16:21-22).

    2. Paul told Timothy that he had imparted to him certain gifts through the laying on of hands (I Timothy 4:14; compare Romans 1:11).

C. Confirmation — Through the laying on of hands one party confirms, or renders, the other party more firm. In other words, there is a strengthening that takes place.

    1. The priests in the Old Testament would bless the people, lifting their hands toward them (Leviticus 9:22).

    2. New Testament believers were confirmed, or rendered more firm, by the laying on of the hands of the leadership (Acts 14:22).

IV. WHAT ARE THE WAYS IN WHICH WE CAN SEE THE LAYING ON OF HANDS OPERATING IN THE NEW TESTAMENT CHURCH?

A. The laying on of hands is often used in connection with _____ .

    1. In the ministry of Jesus (Luke 4:40).

    2. In the ministry of the apostles (Acts 5:12).

    3. In Paul's ministry (Acts 28:8).

    4. In the life and ministry of all believers (Mark 16:18).

B. The laying on of hands is used in _____ (Acts 9:17; 19:6).

C. The laying on of hands is used in connection with the impartation of _____

_____ (II Timothy 1:6, 14; I Timothy 4:14).

D. The laying on of hands often functions in connection with _____
(I Timothy 1:18; 4:14).

E. The laying on of hands is used _____
(Mark 10:16).

F. The laying on of hands is used in the _____ of ministries
(Acts 13:2-3).

G. The laying on of hands is used by leadership in connection with the confirmation, appointment or ordination of various ministries (Acts 6:6).

V. WHAT CAUTIONS SHOULD BE EXERCISED IN CONNECTION WITH THE LAYING ON OF HANDS?

There are several cautions that are found in regard to the ministry of the laying on of hands.

A. This is not something to be taken lightly or done suddenly. Because the act of laying on of hands is more than a mere outward symbol and there is, in fact, an impartation to and identification with the candidate, we must be very cautious in our use of this ministry.

B. In every case, except in regard to healing, it was always the leadership who laid hands on the people. Perhaps because of the serious nature of many of these things, the novice is excluded from operating in such ministry.

Conclusion: We can expect that all of the uses of the laying on of hands found in the New Testament will find a place in the Church today. As the Church of Jesus Christ begins to partake of some of the rich inheritance that has been given us in Christ, we will begin to operate with power in spiritual realms. As we begin to use the tools that God has given us, we will see new hope for accomplishing the mission of the Church. God has not given us an impossible command; but the only way the commission will be realized is as we use the equipment that God has provided for the task. The weapons of our warfare are not carnal, but they are mighty! God is concerned that we war a good warfare (I Timothy 1:18).

Church Discipline

Purpose: The purpose of this lesson is to help believers to see the need for discipline in the family of God and that discipline is not something to be feared by the godly, but a means of positive growth and change in the life of every believer.

Key Verse: "All scripture is given by inspiration of God, and is profitable for doctrine, for reproof, for correction, for instruction in righteousness." II Timothy 3:16 KJV

I. WHAT IS THE FOUNDATION FOR DISCIPLINE IN THE CHURCH?

The foundation for discipline in the Church comes from two important instructions given to us by Jesus Himself.

A. Jesus gave a commission to the Church that involves making followers of Christ into "disciplined ones", or disciples.

"Go ye therefore, and teach all nations, baptizing them in the name of the Father, and of the Son, and of the Holy Ghost: Teaching them to observe all things whatsoever I have commanded you: and, lo, I am with you alway, even unto the end of the world." Matthew 28:19-20 KJV

B. Jesus gave instructions to the Church as to how to handle difficulties that arise between members of the Church.

"Moreover if thy brother shall trespass against thee, go and tell him his fault between thee and him alone: if he shall hear thee, thou hast gained thy brother. But if he will not hear thee, then take with thee one or two more, that in the mouth of two or three witnesses every word may be established. And if he shall neglect to hear them, tell it unto the church: but if he neglect to hear the church, let him be unto thee as an heathen man and a publican. Verily I say unto you, Whatsoever ye shall bind on earth shall be bound in heaven: and whatsoever ye shall loose on earth shall be loosed in heaven." Matthew 18:15-18 KJV

II. WHY IS DISCIPLINE NECESSARY?

A. Discipline is necessary for order in the House of God (Colossians 3:5) and for producing order in the lives of people.

 1. It has the potential for bringing about change and growth in the life of an individual when nothing else will (Titus 1:13).

 2. It prohibits the leavening influence of sin from gaining a foothold in other members of the congregation (I Corinthians 5:6).

 3. It counteracts the spirit of lawlessness in our age (I Timothy 1:9).

 4. It helps the individual member deal with sin in himself that, by himself, he has been unable to eliminate (Galatians 6:1-2).

 5. It underscores the value of righteousness as the basis for all relationships in the Body.

B. Without discipline some very negative things result.

 1. Without discipline there is no clear standard of right and wrong among the people (I Corinthians 5:1-2).

 2. Without discipline sinning members go on sinning, destroying their own potential fruitfulness in God.

 3. Without Church discipline there is the potential for others to do outwardly what they have only been tempted to do inwardly (unjudged activity is a tacit approval of it).

 4. Without Church discipline the spiritual life of the Body, as a whole, becomes greatly weakened.

 5. Without Church discipline, confidence and respect for the Church leadership is lost.

III. WHAT BIBLICAL WORDS ARE USED IN CONNECTION WITH DISCIPLINE IN THE BIBLE?

Church discipline does not simply involve removal from fellowship of the sinning person. Discipline may ultimately lead to such an action, but many words are used in the New Testament to describe the kind of appeals that should be made to the person who calls himself a Christian but who maintains a sinful lifestyle.

A. _____ . To convict, to expose by conviction, to bring light, to admonish, to correct, to call to account, to show one his fault (demanding an explanation), to chasten, to punish (II Timothy 4:2).

B. _____ . To tax with a fault, chide, reprove, censure severely (II Timothy 4:2).

C. _____ . To warn, disapprove or exhort (I Thessalonians 5:12).

D. _____ . To restore to an upright or right state, to raise up again, to reform, to restore, to reestablish (II Timothy 3:16).

E. _____ . To separate, put asunder, to select, to approve, to determine, to decree, to judge, to pronounce an opinion concerning right and wrong, to rule, to govern, to preside over with power of giving judicial decisions (I Corinthians 5:3, 12-13).

IV. *WHAT AREAS OF MISCONDUCT REQUIRE BIBLICAL DISCIPLINE?*

The problems for which discipline is made necessary fall into three main categories.

A. _____ . When two people who claim to be Christians willfully refuse to be reconciled, they are putting themselves in a place of discipline (Matthew 18:15; II Corinthians 6:14-18).

B. _____ . When a person persistently teaches false and damaging doctrines, he is to be disciplined (Romans 16:17; Titus 3:10-11).

C. _____ . When a person who claims to be a Christian leads a life of sin, immorality or disorderliness he is to be disciplined (I Corinthians 5:11; II Thessalonians 3:6).

V. *WHAT IS THE SCRIPTURAL PROCEDURE FOR DISCIPLINE?*

In Matthew 18:15-20, Jesus gave a guideline concerning the stages of Church discipline. He gave four steps. Normally, the first step is the only step that will be necessary in the life of a sincere believer. The refusal of the person being disciplined to align themselves with the Word of God at any point always forces them to move to the next level.

A. The problem is handled on a personal level.

B. If there is no response, two or three are to confront the individual (preferably those in leadership).

C. If there is no response, the church (or eldership) as a whole is to get involved.

D. If there is no response, the person is to be removed from membership in the church by the leadership of the church.

VI. *WHAT IS TO BE THE ATTITUDE OF A RESTORER?*

The attitude of those exercising discipline is very important.

A. He must be motivated by love (Hebrews 12:6; Revelation 3:19; Ephesians 4:15).

B. He must do it with gentleness (I Thessalonians 2:1-9, Psalms 141:5).

C. He must have a spirit of meekness (Galatians 6:1-2).

D. He must be ready to extend mercy and forgiveness (II Corinthians 2:6-8).

E. He must have the heart of a father (I Thessalonians 2:10-12).

F. He must reprove in wisdom (Proverbs 25:12).

VII. *WHAT ARE THE THREE MAIN PURPOSES OF CHURCH DISCIPLINE?*

A. To maintain the _____ of _____
(Romans 2:24).

B. To maintain the _____ of _____
of the Church (Ephesians 5:27).

C. To _____ the repentant believer (Galatians 6:1; II Corinthians 2:7-10).

Conclusion: Discipline is a normal part of family life. It is demonstration of faithfulness and is designed for the restoration and salvation of God's people. It is a means of instruction and grace, not destruction. It is an evidence of love, not hate or fear. The believer who sees discipline in this way will not despise it but learn to embrace it as an instrument in their life to greater productivity in the Kingdom of God (Proverbs 15:10).

Local Church Commitment

Purpose: The purpose of this lesson is to help the believer see the need to be committed to and actively involved in a specific local church if they are to realize their full potential in Christ, become mature in their personal growth and development and find full release and expression in the ministry that has been given to them by Christ.

Key Verse: "Now therefore ye are no more strangers and foreigners, but fellow-citizens with the saints, and of the household of God; and are built upon the foundation of the apostles and prophets, Jesus Christ himself being the chief cornerstone; in whom all the building fitly framed together groweth unto an holy temple in the Lord: in whom ye also are builded together for an habitation of God through the Spirit." Eph. 2:19-22 KJV

I. WHAT DOES THE WORD "COMMITMENT" MEAN?

The word "commitment" itself does not occur in the King James version of the Bible, but when we understand the meaning of this word, we find that it is a concept that occurs throughout the Bible and is the basis for the entering into and maintaining all covenants.

A. To be committed to someone is to cleave to, to adhere to, to be attached to, to join oneself closely to or to stick to the side of another.

B. In the Greek language, the concept of commitment implied a gluing together, a firm fastening and a giving of oneself steadfastly to another.

II. IN WHAT AREAS DOES GOD TEACH US COMMITMENT?

A. God wants us to be committed, firmly attached and joined closely to _____

_____ (Acts 11:23; I Corinthians 6:17).

B. God wants everyone to be committed to the _____
as a foundation for our life (Psalms 119:31).

C. God wants _____ to be bound together
closely in a strong covenant relationship (Gen. 2:24).

D. God wants believers in Christ to be committed to _____ in the Body
of Christ (Ephesians 4:1-6, 16).

III. WHAT ILLUSTRATIONS OF THE CHURCH DOES GOD GIVE US TO HELP US UNDERSTAND THE IMPORTANCE OF OUR COMMITMENT?

God uses many means to teach us commitment. There are three main concepts God links with the church to help us understand how we fit in with one another.

A. The Church is a _____ composed of living stones that are built, or fitly framed, together (Ephesians 2:19-22; I Peter 2:5). As stones in a building, we are to stand along side some stones, come under the authority of other stones and provide covering and protection for others. If any stone is out of place, the walls of the temple will be incomplete and vulnerable.

B. The Church is a _____ composed of individual members that are interlocked and vitally linked to each other (Ephesians 4:16; I Corinthians 12:20, 27). As members of the body we must be in our place and functioning in harmony and peace with other members of the body if the body is to fulfill its purpose and perform effectively.

C. The Church is a _____ made up of many brothers and sisters (Ephesians 3:15; Galatians 6:10). Each member of that family has a responsibility to watch and care for other members of the family to see others fulfilled and growing in their relationship to the Heavenly Father.

IV. WHAT WAYS DO WE DEMONSTRATE COMMITMENT TO ONE ANOTHER?

The Bible lists many responsibilities that Christians have one to another. Every believer must measure their body relationships according to these guidelines.

A. There are many things Christians do toward one another because of this commitment.

1. They love one another (I Peter 1:22).

2. They comfort one another (I Thessalonians 4:18).

3. They exhort one another (Hebrews 10:25).

4. They build up one another (Romans 14:19).

5. They admonish one another (Colossians 3:16).

6. They serve one another (I Peter 4:10).

7. They forgive one another (Ephesians 4:32).

8. They submit to one another (Ephesians 5:21).

9. In addition, they pray for one another, bear one another's burdens, have compassion one to another and are kindly affectioned one to another.

B. There are many things Christians do not do to each other because of this commitment.

   1. They do not condemn or criticize each other (Romans 14:13).

   2. They do not go to law with each other (I Corinthians 6:7).

   3. They do not speak evil of one another (James 4:11).

   4. They do not envy one another (Galatians 5:26).

   5. They do not hurt or do anything that would harm another (Galatians 5:15).

V. HOW IS OUR COMMITMENT EXPRESSED IN A LOCAL CHURCH?

God not only wants us to relate these truths to our relationship to the worldwide Body of Christ, but He wants us to demonstrate a commitment to a local family or body of believers. When a person is committed to a local assembly it means several things.

A. It means that he is committing himself to a specific church family (Psalms 68:1-6).

B. It means that he is willing to support the vision and direction of that family.

C. It means that he is willing to come under the authority in that family (Hebrews 13:17).

D. It means that he is willing to give his time and energy to that family.

E. It means that he is committed to the gathering times of that family.

F. It means that he is committed to the financial support of that family.

G. It means that he is committed in a special way to the members of that family.

H. It means that he is willing to bear the burdens of that family.

VI. IS THERE A NEED TO VERBALIZE OUR COMMITMENTS?

Yes! Verbalizing commitments actually confirms them or renders them more firm.

A. This is true in marriage in the exchanging of vows.

B. This has always been true in various relational commitments in the Bible.

   1. Joshua before Israel

      "As for me and my house, we will serve the Lord." Joshua 24:15

   2. Ruth unto Naomi

      "For whither thou goest, I will go; and where thou lodgest, I will lodge: thy people shall be my people, and thy God my God." Ruth 1:16

Conclusion: God is showing His Body the need for being committed in these days. Every general commitment to Christ and His Church, however, must manifest itself in a specific commitment to a place or it is a false commitment. To say you are committed to what God is doing in a general way and not identify with a local church in a specific way is to dwell carelessly and it could lead to deception. For a child to do this in the natural — to say that he belonged to the great family of mankind but refused to identify with a specific natural family — would seem ridiculous. Yet, how many of God's people desiring to identify with the universal Body of Christ and Family of God have refused to identify and commit themselves to a specific local assembly? God help us to have the courage to make steadfast commitments in these days.

Church Membership

Purpose: The purpose of this lesson is to help the believer see that membership in a specific local church is not to be feared but something that will be beneficial to him in walking out his commitment to the Lord and other members of the body of Christ.

Key Verse: "Again I say unto you, that if two of you shall agree on earth as touching any thing that they shall ask, it shall be done for them of my Father which is in Heaven. For where two or three are gathered together in my name, there am I in the midst of them." Matthew 18:19-20 KJV

I. IS THE CHURCH OF JESUS CHRIST MEANT TO BE AN EXCLUSIVE GROUP?

When properly understood, it is true that the Church is meant to be exclusive.

A. The word "church" in the Greek language means "called out ones". The Church of Jesus Christ is to consist of only those who are called out of the world by the Gospel of Jesus Christ. It consists of those whose citizenship is in heaven (Philippians 3:20).

B. Church membership is exclusive; however, it is also clear that church attendance is to be open to all (I Corinthians 14:23; James 2:2-4).

II. WAS THE NEW TESTAMENT CHURCH CONSCIOUS OF THE NUMBER OF PEOPLE WHO WERE ADDED TO THEM?

Yes. It is very clear in the Gospels and the book of Acts that the disciples and the early believers were actually numbered and accounted for.

A. Jesus chose 12 apostles who were named and numbered (Luke 9:1, 12).

B. Jesus later chose 70 others as His own (Luke 10:1-2).

C. Over 500 brethren saw Jesus in His ascension (I Corinthians 15:3-8).

D. Before Pentecost, 120 disciples gathered in the upper room (Acts 1:15).

E. There were added unto them (the 120) about 3000 souls (Acts 2:41, 47).

F. About 5000 believed and were added to the church (Acts 4:4).

G. The number of the disciples multiplied greatly in Jerusalem (Acts 6:7).

III. *IS IT SCRIPTURAL TO HAVE SOME KIND OF CHURCH ROLL OR RECORDS?*

Yes! The Old Testament and New Testament refer to books where the names of God's people were kept for records. It would be impossible to fully take care of God's sheep if no one knew where they were or if they really belonged to some local church.

A. Old Testament

1. The Israelites had their names in the Books of Geneology of the Nation. They were numbered before the Lord (Numbers 1-2).

2. The Levites were also numbered before the Lord before they could minister in the priestly offices (Numbers 3).

3. Every one numbered in Israel had to be redeemed with silver (Exodus 30:11-16).

4. The remnant from Babylon had to be registered in the book in order to minister in the priesthood (Ezra 2:62, 63; Nehemiah 7).

B. New Testament

1. The Church of the Firstborn have their names written in heaven (Hebrews 12:22-24).

2. The redeemed of all ages have their names also written in the Book of Life (Philippians 4:3; Revelation 13:8; 17:8; 20:12-15; 21:27).

God keeps records! God keeps the names and numbers of the saints in His roll! If God Himself does this, then there should be no problem if finite man does likewise! God knows who is in His book and who is not.

IV. *HOW DOES ONE BECOME A MEMBER OF CHRIST'S CHURCH?*

There are two aspects to Church membership in the book of Acts.

A. Spiritual membership.

You do not become a member by signing up, taking a pledge or subscribing to a particular set of doctrines. In the early church you had to be added to the *Lord,* which involved a spiritual experience of coming into right relationship with and under the lordship of Jesus Christ as personal Savior (Acts 5:14; 11:24). Spiritual membership is foundational to all other experiences in God.

B. Practical membership.

There must also be a visible and practical expression of Church membership as seen in the Book of Acts. This is seen in belonging to "the church local". Believers that were added to the Lord were also added to the Church, which is His Body (Acts 2:41, 47).

In the New Testament, all members of the universal Church were also members of the Local Church. Any idea of enjoying salvation or being a Christian in isolation is foreign to the New Testament. Fellowship with Christ includes fellowship with His Body (I John 1:3, 6-7; I Corinthians 1:9).

V. WHY DO SOME PEOPLE HAVE PROBLEMS WITH CHURCH MEMBERSHIP?

There are many reasons why some people have rejected the concept of church membership.

A. Some have a fear of _____ . Because they have been hurt in the past by a misuse or abuse of membership, they are now very cautious about such commitments.

B. Some do not want to be _____ . Because they want the freedom to move and operate without accountability to human authority, they do not see church membership fitting into their plan for life.

C. Some do not believe it is _____ . Because there are no direct commands concerning membership, they feel that God must be opposed to official membership.

VI. WHAT ARE SOME ADVANTAGES OF PRACTICAL CHURCH MEMBERSHIP?

A. _____ (Colossians 2:2). Deeper levels of fellowship and family relationships are able to be developed.

B. _____ (I Corinthians 12:12-27). A greater sense of belonging and worth can develop among members.

C. _____ (Ephesians 4:16). We have a greater productivity and impact in the lives of other members.

D. _____ (Galatians 6:1-2). There is a greater sense of accountability and responsibility among members.

E. _____ (I Thessalonians 5:12). There is greater opportunity to receive consistent pastoral care and oversight.

F. _____ (Deuteronomy 32:30). There is a greater release of power as believers bind themselves together for a common goal.

G. _____ (Matthew 18:19-20). God promises a greater release of His presence in the corporate assembly.

VII. WHAT IMPORTANT QUESTIONS SHOULD EVERY BELIEVER ANSWER IN REGARD TO CHURCH MEMBERSHIP?

Anyone who is a Christian and claims to be part of Christ needs to face the following questions realistically.

A. Who is over me in the Lord (Hebrews 13:17)?

B. When I was added to the Lord, in what way was I added to the Church (Acts 2:41, 42)?

C. When I gather together with the disciples, with whom do I gather (Acts 20:7)?

D. With whom am I allowing God to perfectly join me (I Corinthians 1:10)?

Conclusion: Every true believer in Christ must consider the question of church membership. All of the dynamics of the Christian life must be worked out in the context of others of like faith. The local church is God's vehicle through which He would strengthen and equip His people. To reject the local church is to resist God's plan and elevate ourselves above God. We need the Lord, but we also need each other if we are going to become all that God desires of us.

25

The Body of Christ

Purpose: The purpose of this lesson is to help each believer see that he has an important place of function and ministry that no one else can fulfill and that it is absolutely necessary for the purposes of God to be fulfilled for each member of the Body to be actively involved in that ministry.

Key Verse: "I beseech you therefore, brethren, by the mercies of God, that ye present your bodies a living sacrifice, holy, acceptable unto God, which is your reasonable service. And be not conformed to this world: but be ye transformed by the renewing of your mind, that ye may prove what is that good, and acceptable, and perfect, will of God. For I say, through the grace given unto me, to every man that is among you, not to think of himself more highly than he ought to think; but to think soberly, according as God hath dealt to every man the measure of faith. For as we have many members in one body, and all members have not the same office: so we, being many, are one body in Christ, and every one members one of another." Romans 12:1-5 KJV

I. WHAT DOES THE PICTURE OF THE BODY OF CHRIST HELP US TO UNDER-STAND CONCERNING THE NATURE OF THE CHURCH?

A. The Church as the Body of Christ has one Head, Jesus Christ (Ephesians 5:24).

    1. Christ is to be the sovereign authority in the Church (Ephesians 5:24).

    2. Christ is the source of life to the Body (Colossians 1:18; 2:11-13).

    3. Christ is the sustainer of the life of the Body (Colossians 2:19).

B. The Church as the Body of Christ has many members (I Corinthians 12:20).

    1. Each member is vitally connected to the other members (Ephesians 2:13; I Corinthians 12:13).

    2. Each member is to function at the direction of the Head (Ephesians 1:21, 22; 4:15-16).

3. Each member is totally dependent on the other members (I Corinthians 12:21, 22, 26).

4. Each member has an important place of function (I Corinthians 12:27).

II. WHAT HAS GOD GIVEN TO THE MEMBERS OF THE BODY OF CHRIST TO INSURE ITS GROWTH, HEALTH AND PROSPERITY?

A. God has given natural abilities and talents that are to be used for His glory (Matthew 25:14-20).

B. God has, by His Spirit, given spiritual gifts that are to be operating in the House of the Lord (I Corinthians 12:7, 11).

C. God has given each member of the Body a ministry, or function, that adds to the edification of the whole (I Corinthians 12:28).

1. These ministries all find their origin in the Lord Jesus Christ.

2. These ministries are merely an expression of Christ in you (Colossians 1:27).

3. These ministries, functioning together, will make up, or comprise, the fullness of Christ (Ephesians 1:22-23).

III. WHAT IS NECESSARY IF THE CHURCH IS GOING TO FULFILL, OR COMPLETE, THE MINISTRY OF THE LORD JESUS CHRIST?

If the Church as the Body of Christ is to fulfill its ministry as God intended, each member is going to have to recognize and receive the ministry of others. This means several things:

A. The members of the Body must recognize that they are members one of another (I Corinthians 12:7-27).

B. The members of the Body must be at peace with one another (Mark 9:50).

C. The members of the Body must seek the interest of the other members (Hebrews 10:24-25).

D. The members of the Body will always seek to strengthen, or edify, other members (Romans 14:19).

IV. WHAT DO I NEED TO DO TO FIND MY PLACE IN THE BODY OF CHRIST?

A. Recognize that you personally have an important place of function and _____

_____ before the Lord (I Corinthians 12:7, 11, 18).

B. Recognize that God has made you _____ to the ministry to which He has called you (Ephesians 2:10).

C. Recognize that it is God who equips you with_____ necessary to fulfill your ministry (Romans 12:3-6; I Peter 4:10).

D. Recognize the headship of Jesus Christ and be _____ Him in all things (Ephesians 1:21-23; 4:15; 5:23).

E. Recognize that all ministry equals and begins with _____ (Luke 22:26-27).

F. Recognize the area of _____ which God is calling you (Romans 12:3-5).

G. Recognize that no one ministry is _____ than another (I Corinthians 12:21, 25).

H. Recognize that all ministry develops over a _____

_____ (Psalms 75:5-6).

I. Recognize that we will only be as successful as we are willing to _____

_____ apply ourselves (Romans 12:1, 2, 10).

J. Recognize that God is going to give you _____ or divine enablement to do His will (Philippians 2:13).

Conclusion: God has called a Body of people to flow together in harmony and unity to fulfill a common goal and purpose. That Body is the Church of Jesus Christ, which is composed of individuals who have answered the call of the Gospel, who have joined themselves together under the Lordship of Jesus Christ and who have laid down their wills to do God's eternal will. It is this Body that is going to fulfill and complete the ministry of Christ on earth today.

"Now may the God who gives the power of patient endurance (steadfastness) and Who supplies encouragement, grant you to live in such mutual harmony and such full sympathy with one another, in accord with Christ Jesus, that together you may (unanimously) with united hearts and one voice, praise and glorify the God and Father of our Lord Jesus Christ, the Messiah."

Romans 15:5-6 (Amplified)

Study Questions

Lessons 17-25

LESSON 17 — THE CHURCH

1. It is in the local church that we are going to put our _____

   _____ into practice.

2. The Church that Christ is building today will (1) _____ ,

   (2) _____ , (3) _____ ,

   (4) _____ , and (5) _____ .

LESSON 18 — RESTORATION OF THE CHURCH

3. The word ''restoration'' means to _____

   _____

   _____ .

4. When this term is applied to the Church, it refers to _____

   _____ .

LESSON 19 — THE HOME

5. The key passage that describes the role and function of the man in the home is _____

   _____ and the key passage describing the woman's role is

   _____ .

6. The five keys to successful family living include (1) _____

   _____ , (2) _____ ,

   (3) _____ , (4) _____ ,

   and (5) _____ .

LESSON 23 — LOCAL CHURCH COMMITMENT

13. To be committed to someone is to _____

    _____

    _____ .

14. Every general commitment to Christ and His Church must manifest itself in a _____

    _____ .

LESSON 24 — CHURCH MEMBERSHIP

15. In the New Testament, all members of the universal Church were also members _____

    _____ .

16. Some advantages of practical church membership include:

    (1) _____   (5) _____

    (2) _____   (6) _____

    (3) _____   (7) _____

    (4) _____

LESSON 25 — THE BODY OF CHRIST

17. God has given each membeh of the Body _____

    _____ that adds to the edification of the whole.

18. If the Church, as the Body of Christ, is to fulfill its ministry as God intended, each member is going to

    have to _____

    _____ .

LESSON 1

I.   A.   teaching;
          instruction
II. A.   good works
     B.   an effective
     C.   firmly
     D.   express love
     E.   properly function
III. A.   deception
     B.   teach and instruct
     C.   an answer;
          an answer to every man
     D.   our destiny
IV. A.   sound
     B.   pure
     C.   Scripture
     D.   faith
     E.   practiced

LESSON 2

I.   —   "repent";
          "believe"
     A.   repentance
     B.   repentance
     C.   repentance
     D.   repentance
     E.   repentance
II. A.   heart;
          attitude
     B.   excuses and apologies
             for sin
III. A.   fall of Adam
     B.   every individual
     C.   in himself
IV. A.   Conviction of sin
     B.   Worldly sorrow
     C.   Mere reformation
     D.   Being religious
     E.   Mental faith

LESSON 3

I.   B.   dependent
     C.   faith
III. A.   the Word of God
     B.   a condition of the heart;
          only
IV. A.   confession
     B.   obedience
V.   A.   promise
     B.   conditions
     C.   delay
VI. A.   true
     B.   hearing
     C.   doers
     D.   Exercise
     E.   Avoid

LESSON 4

I.   —   immersed
III. A.   Repentance
      B.   Faith
IV.   A.   identified;
           newness
      B.   victory
      C.   cleansing
      D.   the name
      E.   heart
V.   A.   put off
      B.   self
      C.   a new beginning
      D.   a new name
VI.   A.   immersion
      B.   the name
VII. A.   A farewell
      B.   A new standard
      C.   A disciple

LESSON 5

III. —   YES
V. A.   promise
   B.   power
   C.   definite
   D.   subsequent to
   E.   foundation
VI. A.   tongues
   B.   speech or utterance
   C.   tongues
   D.   tongues;
      —   speaking with tongues
VII. —   All believers
VIII. A.   before
   B.   Ask Jesus
   C.   not doubting
   D.   speaking
   E.   daily

LESSON 6

I. A.   To evangelize
   B.   To make disciples
   C.   To be witnesses
   D.   To feed others
II. A1   taught;
          trained
   B3   Orderly conduct
III. A.   Lord
   B.   taught
   C.   respond
   D.   corrected
IV. A.   home
   B.   family
   C.   occupation
   D.   possessions;
          be willing
V. —   better
VI. A.   strong
   B.   Christ
   C.   follow
   D.   minister
   E.   good and faithful

LESSON 7

I. A.   "the act of using a thing
          in common"
   B.   communion
II.   two directions
   A.   God-ward
   B.   man-ward
III. —   shall all men know
IV. —   separation
V. A.   Doctrinal concerns
   B.   Disorderly conduct
   —   eat;
          keep company (fellowship)

LESSON 8

I. A.   Supper
   B.   Table;
          Table
   C.   communion
   D.   bread
IV. A.   remembrance
   B.   communion
   C.   unity
   D.   love
   E.   healing
   F.   examination
   G.   thanksgiving
   H.   blessing
   I.   witness

LESSON 9

- IV. A. faith
  - B. humbly
  - C. will
  - D. pure
  - E. hypocrisy
- V. A. all
  - B. daily
  - C. listening
- VII. A. Individually
  - B. With two or three
  - C. Corporately

LESSON 10

- III. A. life
  - B. time
  - C. talents and abilities
  - D. possessions
  - E. finances
- VI. A. lose it
  - B. increase
  - C. wisdom
  - D. accountability
  - E. industrious
  - F. slothful
  - G. Faithfulness

LESSON 11

- III. A. tenth
  - C. all we have
  - D. covetousness
  - E. beginning
- V. A. ourselves
  - B. willingly
  - C. cheerfully
  - D. generously
  - E. proportionately
  - F. regularly
  - G. systematically
  - H. lovingly
  - I. thankfully
  - J. sacrificially
  - K. ministry

LESSON 12

- II. A. natural
  - B. mental and emotional
  - C. spiritual
- VI. C1 prayer
  - 2 hands
  - 3 oil
  - 4 spoken Word
  - 5 table of
  - 6 gifts of
  - 7 ministry of

LESSON 13

- III. B1 yielded
  - 2 desire
  - 3 learn
  - 4 pray
  - 5 faith
  - 6 stir up
- IV. A. building up
  - B1 message
  - 2 time
  - 3 manner

LESSON 14

- II. A. spirit
  - B. truth
- III. A. spontaneous
  - B. heart
  - C. brokenness; humility
  - D. often
  - E. corporate
  - F. praise
- IV. A. voices
  - B. hands
  - C. posture

LESSON 15

- I. — good news
- II. C. in sin
  - 1 wrath
  - 2 condemnation
  - 3 death
  - 4 dead
  - 5 alienated
  - 6 hostile
  - D. darkness
- III. B1 righteous
  - 2 no
  - 3 image of God
  - 4 peace
  - 5 access
- IV. A. preached
  - B. Church
  - C. All believers

LESSON 16

- IV. A. Praying regularly
  - B. honor and respect
  - C. Submitting
  - D. Voting
  - E. Paying taxes
  - F. expressing concerns
  - G. public issues
  - H. political system

LESSON 17

- IV. C1a heritage
  - 1b arrows
  - 1c olive
  - 1d reward
  - 1e crown

LESSON 18

- I. A. building;
         called out;
         separated;
         gathered together
- III. A. covenant commitment
- V. A. holy
  - B. unified
  - C. victorious
  - D. dominion
  - E. fulness of Christ

LESSON 19

- II. A1 powerful
  - 2 truth
  - 3 character
  - B1 first love
  - 2 supernatural
  - 3 Spirit
  - 4 compromise
- IV. A. more

LESSON 20

- II. A. government
  - 2 rule
  - B. elders
  - 2 plurality of elders
  - 2a one
  - b chief elder
  - 3 bishop
  - C1 character
  - 2 spiritual vision
  - 3 houses in order
  - 4 gifted and skilled
- III. A. Ruling
  - B. Shepherding
  - C. Instructing

LESSON 21

   II. A.   power
        B.   power
  IV. A.   healing
        B.   confirming the Holy Ghost
        C.   spiritual gifts
        D.   prophecy
        E.   to impart a blessing
        F.   sending out

LESSON 22

  III. A.   Reprove
        B.   Rebuke
        C.   Admonish
        D.   Correct
        E.   Judge
  IV. A.   Personal Relationships
        B.   Doctrinal Areas
        C.   Areas of Practice
 VII. A.   honor;
             God
        B.   holiness;
             purity
        C.   restore

LESSON 23

   II. A.   Himself
        B.   Word of God
        C.   husbands and wives
        D.   each other
  III. A.   temple
        B.   body
        C.   family

LESSON 24

   V. A.   being hurt
        B.   tied down
        C.   scriptural
  VI. A.   Fellowship
        B.   Fulfillment
        C.   Fruitfulness
        D.   Accountability
        E.   Growth
        F.   Power
        G.   Presence of God

LESSON 25

  IV. A.   responsibility
        B.   perfectly suited
        C.   the gifts
        D.   subject to
        E.   service
        F.   service to
        G.   more important
        H.   period of time
        I.   sacrificially
        J.   special grace

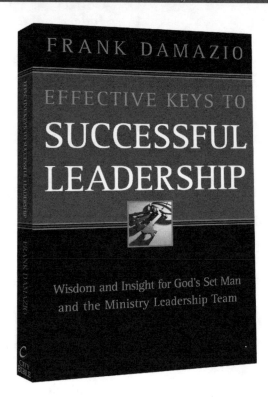

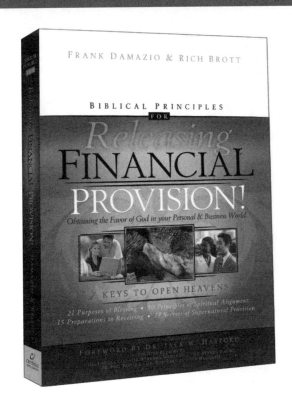

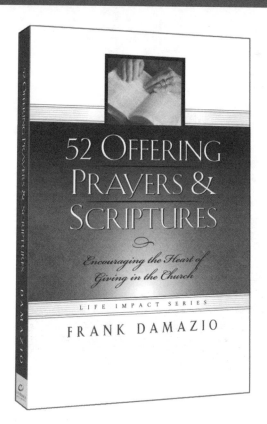

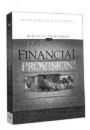

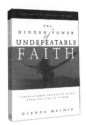

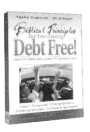

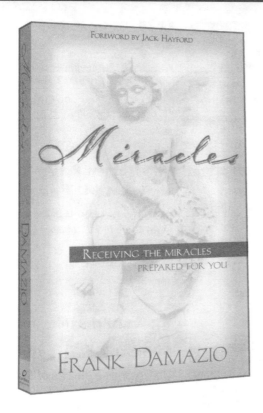

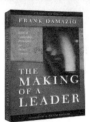

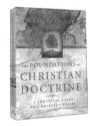

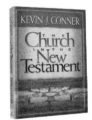

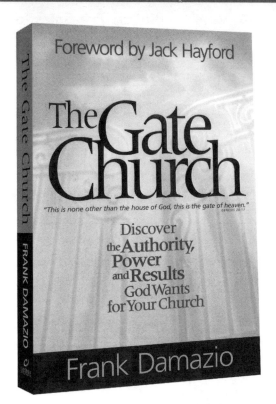